"It has been my privilege [...] now learning from Dr. Jef[...] Sunday school at Independent Presbyterian [...] Jeff is a brilliant biblical scholar, but his scholarship is accessible to all of us. He combines excellent scholarship with a commitment to making the Scriptures come to life with examples from not only his own personal history but also from art, literature, poetry, cinema, sports, nature, and current cultural references. He starts from a basis of deep personal faith, but his faith does not shrink from the lived experiences so many of us have of wrestling with doubt and of struggling to find God's presence in the midst of our own grief and pain. This book is no exception. This beautiful guide to the faithful search for God offers practical help as we walk the path of faith. Even as Jeff wrestles with the experience of seeking a sometimes-elusive God, in the end he reaffirms the mystery and the certainty of God's steadfast, loving, challenging presence in our lives and in the world. I am honored to recommend this beautiful book to all who seek a deeper relationship with God and Jesus Christ, whom you will meet in profound ways in these pages."

–The Rev. Susan A. Clayton, associate pastor
Independent Presbyterian Church (PCUSA)
Birmingham, Alabama

"Jeff Leonard writes as a person who has passionately pursued God. Leonard writes with the skill of a scholar and the heart of a sincere seeker, who invites us to embrace and embark upon a journey that often leads to more questions than answers, and more winding curves, than direct pathways as we search for God. *Seekers in the Hands of an Elusive God* is both an intellectual and spiritual treatise that encourages as it informs followers of the Way to 'seek him while he may be found and call on him while he is near.'"

–Tyshawn Gardner, associate professor of preaching
George W. Truett Seminary
Baylor University, Birmingham, Alabama

"*Seekers in the Hands of an Elusive God* presents a captivating and thought-provoking exploration of the tension between God's omnipresent and yet elusive nature. Jeffery Leonard adeptly accompanies readers through a journey of discovery that is both intellectually challenging and spiritually fulfilling. Leonard's Bible-centered approach and carefully chosen texts invite readers to wrestle with a complex theological issue. His accurate and insightful interpretations are beautifully enriched with a variety of extrabiblical material—from ancient Jewish texts to contemporary film and literature—making this book a compelling read for both scholars and laypeople alike. Leonard's reflections offer clarity and comfort, reminding us that God's hiddenness is not an absence but a divine mystery that we are invited to explore and embrace in everyday life. This warm, welcoming book is sure to resonate with all readers, offering both intellectual depth and spiritual reassurance."

–Dr. David Emanuel, adjunct professor
Hebrew Bible and Language
North Central University, Minneapolis, Minnesota

"Jeff Leonard brings the passion, love for the Bible and for others, and even humor to this difficult subject that has made him one of Samford's most beloved professors. Weaving personal stories together with scriptural exegesis, Leonard is an empathetic, insightful, and patient guide in the search for an elusive God."

–Dr. Will Kynes, co-author, *Wrestling with Job:*
Defiant Faith in the Face of Suffering

Seekers in the Hands *of an* Elusive God

JEFFERY M. LEONARD

Seekers in the Hands of an Elusive God

Embracing Hope in Seasons of Darkness

HENDRICKSON PUBLISHERS

Seekers in the Hands of an Elusive God:
Embracing Hope in Seasons of Darkness

© 2025 by Jeffery M. Leonard

Published by Hendrickson Publishers
3 Centennial Drive
Peabody, MA 01960

ISBN 978-1-4964-7618-0 (print)
ISBN 979-8-4005-1146-2 (Kindle ebook)
ISBN 979-8-4005-1148-6 (epub)
ISBN 979-8-4005-1147-9 (Apple epub)

All rights reserved. No part of this book may be reproduced or transmitted in any form or by any means, electronic or mechanical, including photocopying, recording, or by any information storage and retrieval system, without permission in writing from the publisher.

Neither the publisher nor the author is responsible for, nor do they have any control over, the content of any third-party websites cited in this book, whether at the time of the book's publication or in the future.

Cover vector by filo via iStock by Getty Images.

Cover design by Karol Bailey.

Printed in the United States of America

First Printing — April 2025

Library of Congress Control Number: 2024950188

To the memory of my friend,
Jim Barnette
(1961–2021)

There is a place called "heaven" where the good here unfinished is completed; and where the stories unwritten, and the hopes unfulfilled, are continued. We may laugh together yet.

—J. R. R. Tolkien, in a letter to his son Michael, June 9, 1941

Contents

	Acknowledgments	xi
	Introduction	1
1.	An Elusive God	5
2.	Seeking God	17
3.	Seeking God in Scripture	29
4.	Seeking God in Nature	41
5.	Seeking God in Humanity	57
6.	Seeking God in Worship	69
7.	Seeking God in Silence	83
8.	Seeking God in Doubt	97
9.	Seeking God in Suffering	111
10.	Seeking God in Death	129
11.	Seeking God in Joy	147
	Conclusion: Seeking God in Christ	163
	Notes	*171*
	Scripture Index	*181*

Acknowledgments

On a particular Sunday in May 2019, I stood with my friend Jim Barnette on the heights of Mount Arbel and looked out over the Sea of Galilee below. It was a beautiful day. The sky was a piercing blue, and the morning sun threw the surrounding hills into sharp relief along the water's edge. Our group gathered close, and Jim offered us words of encouragement as only he could. Knowing it would be impossible to compete with the vistas clamoring for attention all around us, he told us simply this: He loved us, and he could think of no greater joy than being in that place with that wonderful group of people. Had we known Jim would be taken from us less than two years later, I'm sure we would have tried to hold onto that moment and not let it go. Sadly, we did not know. Our last months with Jim slipped through our hands so quickly that it is still hard to believe he is gone.

All of us who knew Jim have mourned his death in different ways. This book has been part of my own grieving process. It has been my attempt to help others I know have traveled the same hard road I have.

It is for Deanna, whose devotion to her husband was never more evident than in the love she showed Jim in his final months.

It is for Nick and Hannah, who were loved so dearly by their father and who will always carry his memory with them.

It is for the "tribe" at Brookwood Baptist Church who had always supported Jim and his family and who rallied around them so heroically in their most difficult days.

It is for the students in my Studies in Psalms and Wisdom class who braved the book of Job and the psalms of lament even as their hearts were breaking over the departure of their beloved Dr. B.

It is for Emma and Jessica who carried on even when they felt overwhelmed and abandoned, pushed on when they didn't know how, and helped Samford's campus grieve together in our memorial service.

It is for the faculty and students in Samford University's Biblical and Religious Studies department who endured the loss of their professor, colleague, and friend and who continue to honor his memory even today.

It is for the kind souls at Independent Presbyterian Church who patiently endured my first attempts to teach through a version of the material here and who never failed to offer an encouraging word along the way.

It is for my wife, Michaela, who walked with me through the darkest days of this season of struggle. Her love and support never fail.

Lastly, I would be remiss if I did not offer a word of thanks to my colleagues at Hendrickson who helped shepherd this project to completion: My dear friend Jonathan Kline, who encouraged me to pursue the project and helped me get it underway; Kate Walker and Ann Smith, whose meticulous attention to detail caught more errors in my drafts than I care to admit; and Patricia Anders, whose detailed comments, suggestions, and questions made this volume far better than it otherwise would have been.

Introduction

I KNEW FROM THE FIRST SENTENCE of our phone call that something was terribly wrong. Jim Barnette was what I would call a "great soul." He was a big man physically, to be sure, but his frame was hardly big enough to contain his heart. *He loved food.* I couldn't possibly count the times he waxed eloquent over this dish at that place or that dish at the other place. *He loved the Allman Brothers.* It was the rare person who made it five minutes into a conversation with Jim without finding out he knew the band members personally. *He loved his students.* He was a colleague in the department where I teach, and I witnessed firsthand the way he adored his students and the way they adored him right back. *He loved his church.* He poured his heart out in his sermons and held the group so tightly that they affectionately called themselves "the tribe." *He loved his kids.* Hardly a conversation went by without the words "Hannah did this" or "Nick did that." *He loved his wife, Deanna.* He choked back tears when he got to baptize her in the Jordan on a trip we took to Israel. He idolized her. Jim loved so much.

In the summer of 2020, that summer when COVID kept us all so separated from one another, our department chair let us know that Jim was going to be stepping away from classes for the fall. He had suffered a bit of heart trouble a couple of years before, so most of us assumed a flare-up of that sort must have sidelined him for a while. As the weeks went by, though, the tone of our chair's requests for prayer for Jim grew increasingly grave. It was clear that something else was going on. I texted Jim and told him I wasn't sure what was wrong, but he was certainly in my prayers. Almost immediately, he replied, asking if it was a good time to talk. Sure, I said, and gave him a call.

Jim was a masterful speaker, eloquent in every venue where he appeared, but from the first line of our conversation, he struggled to find the right words. He stumbled and stuttered and repeated words multiple times. When he tried to recall the name of the city in Alabama where a significant division of NASA's space program is located—a city exceedingly well known, at least to Alabamians—he said, "It's the place where, you know, the place where, it's the place where, you know, where they have the rockets."

"Huntsville?" I asked, trying to mask my concern.

"Yeah, that's it."

Something much more serious than a heart issue was going on.

In his halting speech, Jim tried to explain that the doctors had found some sort of inflammation in his brain, but they couldn't tell why it was happening. Always one to look on the positive side of things, though, he was happy that his congregation had so many doctors to give him good advice and that he had managed to get an appointment with a specialist who would be sure to help. When the phone conversation ended, I sat in my chair and wept for my friend. What was this man of words going to do with his life when words had now become a stranger to him? In his famous sonnet "On His Blindness," John Milton wrestled with feelings of uselessness now that his sight was gone:

> When I consider how my light is spent
> Ere half my days, in this dark world and wide,
> And that one talent which is death to hide,
> Lodged with me useless, though my soul more bent
> To serve therewith my Maker, and present
> My true account, lest he returning chide.[1]

"That one talent . . . lodged within me useless." This seemed to capture Jim's situation perfectly. To imagine Jim without his voice, without his words—I could hardly bear the thought of it. The only comfort I could find was in knowing that at least there was that specialist who would be able to help.

Unfortunately, there would be no help.

On a Sunday morning in October, Jim announced that he had been diagnosed with what is called Creutzfeldt-Jakob disease. I had heard the name before but had no real idea what it was. Looking it up on the internet, I learned that it was a brain disease caused by some abnormal sort of protein. There was a long list of symptoms on the page, but as I scrolled down, three particular words caught my eye: "Prognosis: Universally fatal." There was no treatment. There were no survivors. My friend would be gone in a matter of months.

More difficult by far than having to work through my own grief over Jim's diagnosis was having to walk through the same process with my students. Nearly all of my students had also been Jim's students at one time or another. Most of them had been mentored by Jim for years as part of a particular program he led for our department. He was professor, pastor, and substitute father to them all at once. No words could suffice to express how grief-stricken my students were. They were devastated.

As it happened, I was teaching a course on Psalms and Wisdom when Jim's condition was announced. Of all places, we were right in the thick of the book of Job. Each new foray into Job's story was an assault on our souls. We could hear in Job's laments echoes of our own laments for Jim. We felt the sting of Job's losses as we reckoned with the certain loss we knew we would soon experience. Worst of all was knowing there was no hope of recovery at the end of our friend's suffering. Job, at least, believed God might one day restore him; there was no hope that God would do the same for Jim. God had never seen fit to heal someone of this disease in the past; he was not going to do so now. Student after student approached me and confessed that this was the hardest part. "I don't know how to pray," one student said. "How do you pray when there is no hope for an answer?"

The days between Jim's diagnosis in October and his death the following February are some of the darkest spiritually I have ever known. In a moment of such terrible need, God seemed to be so far away. I know I am not alone in feeling this sort of spiritual abandonment. I trace the family tree of my ancestors in the faith to souls who cried out:

> Why, O Lord, do you stand far off
>   and hide in times of trouble?
>
> (Ps 10:1)
>
> Why do you sleep, O Lord?
>   Wake up! Do not cast us away forever!
> Why do you hide your face
>   and forget our affliction and distress?
>
> (Ps 44:23–24)
>
> Why do you cast away my soul
>   and hide your face from me?
>
> (Ps 88:14)[2]

There is sorrow and confusion to spare in the many descendant branches of that same family tree. Grief over the loss of a beloved son or daughter. Anguish over abandonment by a faithless father. Heartbreak beyond measure over the torturous decline of a loved one stricken by Alzheimer's. Truthfully, I don't doubt God's existence; the supposedly well-reasoned arguments to the contrary I find generally to be just so tiresome and childish. I don't really doubt God's goodness, either; I know in my heart of hearts that God is good. But I do struggle to find God's presence.

This is a book for those who share my struggle, for those who believe in God and believe God is good but who struggle mightily to understand why God acts as God acts. This is a book for *genuine seekers* who find themselves in the hands of a deliberately *elusive God*.

1

An Elusive God

"For my thoughts are not your thoughts;
 and your ways are not my ways," declares the LORD.
"For as high as the heavens are above the earth,
 so my ways are higher than your ways
 and my thoughts higher than your thoughts."
  (Isa 55:8–9)

And they rose up and drove him out of the town, and they took him to the brow of a hill upon which their town was built in order to throw him off. But passing through their midst, he went on his way.
  (Luke 4:29–30)

Seen or Unseen?

THOSE HARDY ENOUGH TO MAKE IT through all four hours (without commercials!) of Cecil B. DeMille's *The Ten Commandments* will no doubt remember the classic scene in which the fire of God inscribes the words of the Decalogue on a pair of stone tablets. Just as memorable is the scene moments later when Charlton Heston (or is it Moses? Who can tell the difference?) hurls those same tablets down upon the infamous golden calf. In between these two cinematic gems, though, a scene is missing. After Moses receives the Ten Commandments and before the nation's dalliance with the calf, Exodus 24 describes a covenant-sealing ceremony between God and Israel. In the conclusion to what is structured as a long wedding scene, Israel says to God, in effect, "I do"—"All the words that the LORD has spoken, we will do" (v. 3)—and both God and Israel are marked by the blood of the covenant in a manner similar to the way a bride and groom in ceremonies today each receive a wedding ring (vv. 6–8). Then follows one of the most remarkable passages in all of Scripture:

> Then Moses and Aaron, Nadab, and Abihu, and seventy of the elders of Israel ascended, and *they saw the God of Israel*. Under his feet was something like a work of sapphire bricks, clear as the heavens themselves. But God did not stretch out his hand against the nobles of the Israelites. *They beheld God*, and they ate and drank.
>
> (vv. 9–11)

If we look at the Sinai experience as a wedding, it isn't hard to identify the part of the festivities these verses describe; this is the wedding feast that follows the ceremony. But notice the two provocative statements highlighted in these verses: "they saw the God of Israel," and "they beheld God." The underlying Hebrew of the text (*wayyir'û 'ēt 'ĕlōhê yiśrā'ēl* and *wayyeḥĕzû 'et-hā'ĕlōhîm*) could hardly be more clear; not a single word of these phrases is uncertain. The author of the account clearly means to say that the nobles of Israel *saw God himself*. He even remarks on the fact that despite this seeming breach, God did not punish them for doing so. But if this is the case, then what are we to do with a verse like John 1:18 that says, "No one has ever seen God"? John's statement in Greek (*theon oudeis heōraken pōpote*) is just as clear as the Hebrew statement in Exodus. Whatever Exodus 24 might say, John is adamant that no mere human has ever managed to see God.

The authors of Scripture appear to be quite divided on the matter of whether one can actually see God. Exodus 24 certainly says yes, and a great many other passages do so as well. The prophet Ezekiel insists, "I saw visions of God" (Ezek 1:1). Isaiah famously recounts, "I saw the Lord sitting on his throne, high and lifted up" (Isa 6:1). The prophet Micaiah says nearly the same thing: "I saw the LORD, sitting on his throne" (1 Kgs 22:19; cf. 2 Chr 18:18). Amos chimes in with "I saw the Lord standing beside the altar" (Amos 9:1). When Miriam and Aaron challenge Moses' leadership, it is God himself who rebukes the two of them, saying concerning Moses, "I speak to him face to face, plainly and not in riddles. He sees the form of the

Lord" (Num 12:8). And let's not forget that in the Beatitudes, Jesus declares, "Blessed are the pure in heart, for *they shall see God*" (Matt 5:8).

On the other side of the ledger stand various passages that insist *no one* can see God. In addition to John 1:18, there is also John 6:46: "Not that anyone has ever seen the Father except the one who is from God; he is the one who has seen the Father." First John 4:12 adds, "No one has ever seen God," and 3 John 11 says, "The one who does evil has not seen God." Outside of the books traditionally associated with John and his community, there is also 1 Timothy 6:16, which insists concerning the Father, "He alone has immortality, dwelling in unapproachable light, *whom no one has seen nor can see.*" Even within the Torah, the Deuteronomist objects to the notion that the Israelites saw God at Sinai/Horeb:[1]

> You approached and stood at the foot of the mountain as the mountain burned with fire up to the very heart of the heavens. There was darkness, cloud, and gloom. Then the Lord spoke to you from the midst of the fire. You heard the sound of words, *but you did not see any form, only a voice.*
>
> (Deut 4:11–12)

Although Deuteronomy 5:23–28 appears to allude directly to the covenant ceremony described in Exodus 24, it lacks altogether Exodus' language about Moses and the elders' ascending the mountain, seeing God, and eating a meal in his presence. In Deuteronomy's account, the leaders of the people are afraid even to hear the *voice* of God. They cry out:

> And now, why should we die? For this great fire will consume us. If we continue to hear the voice of the Lord our God, we shall die! For who among all flesh has heard the voice of the living God speaking as we have and lived?
>
> (vv. 25–26)

So great is the people's fear that they beg Moses to go and hear the divine voice. There is certainly no thought of their actually being able to see God.

Seeing but Not Seeing All

I'm not convinced that it is altogether necessary to find a way out of this interpretive dilemma. The scholarly side of me is quite comfortable with simply letting the biblical authors stake out their own positions and then finding a way to live in the midst of the resulting tension.

There is one passage, though, a passage that also derives from Sinai, that might shed at least a bit of light on the issue. In the wake of the golden calf incident, Exodus tells us that God threatened to send the Israelites to the promised land *without accompanying them along the way* (Exod 33:3). The prospect of God's abandoning the Israelites in the moment of their greatest need was terrifying. The entire nation went into a state of mourning, and Moses begged God, "If your presence will not go with us, then do not make us go up from here!" (v. 15). If God wasn't going to go with them, then Moses and the people didn't want to go at all.

God finally relented and agreed to accompany the nation. He reassured Moses, "You have found favor in my eyes, and I know you by name" (v. 17). But it was at this point that Moses decided to push the matter one step further. He said to the Lord, "Show me your glory!" (v. 18). Although Moses had already found favor with God, he wanted more. He wanted to see God himself. God's response is fascinating:

> And he said, "I will cause all my goodness to pass before your face, and I will utter the name 'YHWH' before you; I will be gracious to whom I will be gracious, and I will be merciful to whom I will be merciful." And he said, "You are not able to see *my face*, for no one can see me and live." And the Lord said, "Here is a place by me where you may stand on the rock. And it will take place that when my glory passes by, I will put you in the cleft of the rock, and I will cover you with my hand until I have passed by. Then I will remove my hand, and *you may see my back, but my face may not be seen.*
>
> (vv. 19–23)

What God seems to say here is that Moses can *see* God, but he can't see *all* of God. God is *evident* in one sense, but there is another sense in which he remains *elusive*. Apart from Jesus himself, of course, no character in the Bible enjoys a closer relationship with God than Moses. He is the one with whom the Lord spoke "face to face, as a man speaks to his friend" (Exod 33:11). And yet even with Moses, God remained elusive. God spoke to Moses as he did to no one else, but even Moses could see only God's back and not his face. What is true of God's relationship with Moses is true of God's self-revelation elsewhere in Scripture: *Elusiveness* is a fundamental aspect of how God interacts with humanity.

The Tabernacle

One of Israel's most important ways of symbolizing God's presence among his people was through the shrine known as the "tabernacle." In the Torah's priestly accounts, the tabernacle was placed at the very center of the Israelite camp where it served as a perpetual reminder that God was with the people as they traveled through the wilderness.[2] But consider the character of this sacred shrine. The tabernacle wasn't a permanent temple made of blocks and stones, columns and capitals, solid from roof down to foundation. The tabernacle was a tent, a collection of curtains and covers, held up only by poles, and ready to be moved to a new location at a moment's notice. The tabernacle was impermanent, unpredictable, impossible to pin down. *It was a moveable shrine dedicated to an elusive deity.*

And it wasn't just the tent as a whole that marked the elusiveness of Israel's God; the details of the tent and the furnishings associated with it reinforce this idea. Surrounding the tabernacle courtyard was a curtain.[3] Interestingly, although the book of Exodus describes this curtain in great detail, it says nothing about how the panels of the curtain were to be joined, one to another. Apparently, they weren't. Each individual panel of the curtain stood alone, so that the ceaseless wilderness winds could blow through them, creating fleeting separations between one curtain and another. A person standing outside of the tabernacle could catch an endless series of glimpses—but only glimpses—of the work going on inside this sacred area.

If we were to venture into the tabernacle, even then what sights would meet the eye? Mainly smoke and fire. A fire would have been burning almost constantly on the altar in the courtyard, sending smoke from the burnt offerings up to the heavens. Inside the Holy Place—though the likes of us would never be allowed to enter—would be the fire of the menorah's lamps and the smoke of the incense altar. On that one occasion each year when the high priest would enter the actual Holy of Holies itself, even more smoke from the incense altar would be deployed to shield the priest from the burning fire of God's presence (cf. Lev 16). Smoke and fire were the chief symbols of God's presence in the tabernacle, but consider how elusive and impermanent these symbols are. Both can be seen but not held. Their effects are evident, but they cannot be captured. Like the God they symbolize, smoke and fire are elusive, unable to be contained, present but just out of reach.

Present but Just Out of Reach

The elusiveness of God is not a matter tied solely to God's appearance at Sinai or the transient symbols of the tabernacle. Many biblical writers wrestle with God's elusiveness in much more personal terms. In Psalm 10, the psalmist asks of God, "Why do you hide yourself in times of trouble?" (v. 1). He despairs over the way the wicked trample so recklessly over the weak and vulnerable, and he finds more troubling still the fact that they do this, because God seemingly refuses to intervene. In their hearts, the wicked say, "God has forgotten; he has hidden his face; he never sees" (v. 11). The psalmist holds out hope that this isn't the case (v. 14), but in the present moment, he can only plead with God, "Why do you stand far off?" (v. 1).

God's "standing far off" is also the desperate concern of Psalm 22. The famous words that introduce the psalm are witness to the psalmist's struggle with God's seeming absence. He cries out, "My God, my God, why have you forsaken me?" and the lines that follow underscore just how *distant* God remains. In verse 1, he asks why God is "far away" (*rāḥôq*) from saving him. He returns to this theme in verse 11, begging God, "Do not be far (*'al-tirḥāq*) from me!" and again in verse 19, "But you, O LORD, do not be far (*'al-tirḥāq*) from me!" Perhaps reflecting the desperate mental state of the psalmist, Psalm 22 turns repeatedly from the psalmist to God and back to the psalmist. In verse 2, the psalmist's unanswered cries take center stage as he appeals constantly to God but receives no reply:

> O my God, I cry out by day, but you do not answer;
>   by night, but there is no rest for me.

In verse 3, the psalmist turns his focus to God as he unexpectedly offers words of praise:

> But you are holy,
>   enthroned on the praises of Israel.

If this is praise, though, it is praise with a subtle note of criticism. God is described as holy, but the core meaning of the word *holy* (*qādôš*) is to be *separate* or *set apart*. The psalmist doesn't need God to be set apart; he needs him to be *near*. He doesn't need God to be seated on a heavenly throne; he needs God to be present and active in the midst of his troubles.

A similar sort of rebuke in the guise of praise is also evident in verses 4–5:

> In you our ancestors trusted;
> > they trusted, and you rescued them.
> To you they cried out and were saved;
> > in you they trusted and were not put to shame.

That God had delivered the psalmist's ancestors in times gone by only throws into sharp relief the fact that God now refuses to intervene on his behalf. It can't be a matter of *ability* as God had repeatedly demonstrated his might in the past. It could only be a matter of *choice*; God *could* help the psalmist but chooses not to.[4]

For the psalmist, the elusiveness of God moves well beyond the intellectual exercise of distinguishing between full or partial theophanies at Sinai or deciphering the symbolism of the tabernacle and its appurtenances. God's elusiveness is a matter of spiritual (and perhaps physical) desperation:

> Like water, I am poured out;
> > all my bones are out of joint.
> My heart is like wax;
> > it melts inside of me.
> My strength dries up like a potsherd;
> > my tongue sticks to my jaws.
> You have laid me down in the dust of death.
> > > > (vv. 14–15)

We can hardly fail to feel sympathy for a soul in the throes of such deep spiritual agony. This is all the more true for those of us whose own walk of faith is pockmarked with similar seasons of desperation.

Spiritual Desperation

If there is an aspect of the human experience more overwhelming than the feeling of desperation, I hope never to hear about it and pray to God I never have to experience it. For those who have truly felt it, desperation is a state almost impossible to put into words. It's that feeling some of us have had when we've ventured into waters that were too deep and some distress—a cramp, a powerful wave, a faulty piece of scuba gear—has kept us underwater longer than we could hold our breath. There is that moment of sheer panic that hits when we realize we're on the verge of drowning. In an instant, every other concern is banished, and we struggle with a madness that is all-consuming to reach the surface and fill our lungs with one more gasp of air.

I believe my most intense moment of desperation was one that involved my older son, Samuel. When Samuel was eleven, he and I went on a weekend backpacking trip with his Boy Scout troop. After we returned home on Sunday afternoon, he dutifully headed off to take a bath to wash up from the trip. Sometime later, my wife came rushing into my study, screaming that she could not get Samuel to answer her. Given her state of panic, I immediately ran after her to see what was wrong. The door to the small bathroom where Samuel had gone was locked, and though I yelled to him at the very top of my voice, there was no answer. I slammed my hand against the door repeatedly, making a sound so loud that it reverberated through the entire house. Still, though, there was no answer.

There are no words to describe the desperation that overwhelmed us at that moment. What could possibly have happened to our dear son? My mind raced with the prayer "O dear God, no!" and I hurled myself against the door, knocking it off its hinges and sending it crashing into the bathroom. Were it not such a traumatic moment for the two of us, I am sure my wife and I could have laughed at the look of terror on Samuel's face as he finally woke up from what I take to be the soundest sleep any human being has ever experienced. To this day, though, I still can't find the will to laugh about that moment. At the heart of the word *desperation* is the word *despair*, and in that moment, I felt the despair of believing something terrible had happened to my son. I hope I never experience that feeling again.

Desperation isn't limited to physical experiences like nearly drowning or the emotional experience of nearly losing a loved one; there are times when we can also suffer a kind of spiritual desperation. This was certainly the case for the author of Psalm 42. The opening line of the psalm is rightly famous:

> As the deer pants for streams of water,
>   so my soul pants for you, O God.

Here, the psalmist uses the metaphorically rich verb 'āraḡ to describe his spiritual condition; this is a word that describes *panting, craving, longing* for something. Adding to the image is the fact that the word *nep̄eš*, normally translated into English as "soul," is actually a far more physical term in Hebrew; *nep̄eš* refers to a person's *throat*. It is a physical metonymy on par with our use of words like *heart* and *guts* to describe the centers of certain emotions. We say that a person who has courage has guts or that a person who is sad has a broken heart. Here the psalmist's longing for God's presence is vividly described as a kind of desperate thirst for God, akin to the panicked search of a deer for water. This is the image that carries over to the second line of the psalm:

> My *throat* thirsts for God, for the living God;
>   when shall I come and see the face of God?

At the heart of the psalmist's lament is the sense of loss he feels for no longer being able to join in corporate worship. In verse 4, he looks back on a time when he was at the heart of the celebration:

> These things I remember,
>   and I pour out my soul within me:
> How I used to pass through with the throng;
>   I used to lead them to the house of God,
> with a voice of joy and thanks,
>   a multitude making pilgrimage.

It isn't entirely clear why the psalmist can no longer join with the worshiping multitudes. There is a great deal of talk of enemies and adversaries in the psalm (cf. vv. 9–10; 43:1–2).[5] Combined with the psalmist's language of being separated from the temple and altar (cf. v. 6; 43:3–4), perhaps the issue is that the psalmist has been exiled from Jerusalem. Regardless, he now feels the pain of separation from God and from other worshipers.

To many of us, missing a church service might not seem like the end of the world, but there is clearly more to the psalmist's spiritual loneliness than that. A better analogy might be found in something like the loss we feel when we're away from family during the holidays. Most of us are familiar with Bing Crosby's popular standard, "I'll Be Home for Christmas." As the decades have passed, though, it's easy for us to forget that this song was originally recorded in 1943, at the midpoint of America's time in World War II. The words of the song take on a different meaning when we imagine the soldiers and sailors listening to them far away from home at Christmastime:

> I'll be home for Christmas.
> You can plan on me.
> Please have some snow and mistletoe

And presents on the tree.
Christmas eve will find me
Where the love light gleams.
I'll be home for Christmas
If only in my dreams.

Those last two lines in particular highlight the melancholy tone of the song. Being home for Christmas remains just a wish; the only visit home during that wartime Christmas would be one that takes place in a dream.

In Psalm 42, the psalmist's separation from the temple and his once fellow worshipers is compounded by his sense of separation from God. His opponents chide him with the question, "Where is your God?" (v. 3). But more difficult is the question that arises in his own mind: "God, why have you forgotten me?" (v. 9). This is the question that seems to lie at the very heart of spiritual desperation. As the writer laments in Psalm 13:

How long, O Lord, will you forget me forever?
    How long will you hide your face from me?
How long must I bear wounds[6] in my soul,
    pain in my heart all day long?

(vv. 1–2)

There are times when our experience of God's presence is so powerful that it's almost overwhelming: When we see the reflection of God in the work of one of his creatures—a certain painting, a piece of sculpture that seems almost alive, the soaring notes of a piece of music, the interplay of power and fragility of a single voice in song. When we see the reflection of God in some natural vista—the swell of the ocean, the rise of a chain of mountains, the riot of colors in an autumn grove of trees. These are moments when we experience God's presence as powerfully near us, welling up inside of us, undeniable. And then there are those times when God is just so hard to find: When we watch the long, slow decline of a loved one and can find no grace in the suffering they endure. When we suffer the shock of a child's death and can't imagine how we can ever be made whole again. When we see the powerful run roughshod over the weak and can't understand why God doesn't seem to lift a finger to help. These are moments when our faith is pushed to the breaking point. When we want to hold on but don't think we can. When the faintest glimmer of the divine countenance would sustain us, but we see nothing but darkness all around.

Everywhere yet Elusive

The biblical authors assure us that there is nowhere we can go to escape God's presence. Psalm 139 declares:

> Where can I go away from your spirit,
>   where can I flee from your face?
> If I ascend to the heavens, you are there,
>   and if I make my bed in Sheol, there you are.
> If I take the wings of the dawn,
>   if I pitch my tent at the furthermost reaches of the sea,
> even there, your hand leads me,
>   and your right hand takes hold of me.
>
> (vv. 7–10)

The prophet Jeremiah adds:

> "Can a man hide himself in secret places so that I cannot see him?" declares the LORD. "Do I not fill the heavens and the earth?" declares the LORD.
>
> (23:24)

God is everywhere. With the psalmist, we need not worry that we could ever fall outside the reach of God's loving protection. With Jeremiah, we dare not fool ourselves by thinking we could hide our bad deeds from God's vigilant gaze. God is everywhere—and yet God remains elusive. We live within him, and yet sometimes we just can't find him. How can this be? Why is this so?

2

Seeking God

O God, you are my God; I search for you;
  my soul thirsts for you.
My flesh yearns for you
  in a dry and weary land without water.
    (Ps 63:1)

Jacob at Peniel

FEW PASSAGES IN THE BIBLE ARE as unusual as the account of Jacob's nighttime wrestling match in Genesis 32. Because the story is such a familiar one, we're apt to miss the nonchalant way in which the author introduces the narrative: "Jacob was left alone, and a man wrestled with him until the break of dawn" (v. 24). The line is simple enough; simple, that is, until we actually pause to read it. I'm sorry, we might ask, a man did what?

My sons and I have been blessed to take many memorable backpacking trips together. Along the way, we've passed countless fellow hikers—young, old, short, tall, male, female, you name it. We've even had occasion at times to share campsites with other folks along the trail. But in all our travels, we've never been jumped by a stranger who thought it would be a good idea to wrestle with one of us all through the night. And if we did, we certainly wouldn't casually gloss over this fact when we recounted our experiences on our return home.

Unfortunately, the text only gets more confusing as we venture further in. The "man" with whom Jacob wrestles is unable to prevail against the patriarch, yet this same "man" is able to *strike*—or perhaps just *touch* (the Hebrew verb *nāḡaʿ* can mean either)—Jacob on the hip and put it out of joint (v. 25). The man attacks Jacob while he is camping, yet Jacob refuses to let the man go unless he blesses him (v. 26). Jacob is said to wrestle with a man, yet the "man" changes Jacob's name to Israel, saying to him, "You have striven with *God* and with man and have prevailed" (v. 28). And in the end, Jacob names the place Peniel, "Face of *God*," saying "I have seen *God* face to face" (v. 30).

As confusing as it may be, few texts capture the ambiguities of a relationship with God better than this story of Jacob at Peniel. God is powerfully present with Jacob—so powerfully that his experience is described as one of striving *with God*, so powerfully that Jacob claims to have seen God *face to face*. And yet, God remains elusive throughout the narrative. Does Jacob wrestle with God himself or is this *man* merely an angel? (see Hos 12:4–6). If this man is actually God, then why is he unable to prevail against Jacob? If he's just a man, then why does Jacob ask for his blessing? God is engaged but elusive with Jacob; he is present but hidden all at the same time. Most importantly of all, the way Jacob is forced to interact with God is one of *striving, struggling, wrestling*.

Seeking an Omnipresent God

What Scripture presents as such a unique event in the life of Jacob could actually be thought of as a microcosm of all of humanity's interaction with God. We see this, for example, in the way the apostle Paul speaks to the gathered sages at Mars Hill. As Acts 17 describes the scene, Paul arrives in Athens ahead of his companions, Silas and Timothy, and immediately sets about stirring up trouble in town. He debates Jews in the synagogue and Epicureans and Stoics in the marketplace—anyone within ear*shot* was bound to get an ear*ful* of Paul's preaching. When word of Paul's new message reaches some of the leading lights of the city, they haul him in front of the Areopagus to give an account of his teaching. Paul's response to the assembly focuses on the many idols he had seen there:[1]

> Men of Athens, I observe how very religious you are in every way. For as I passed through the city and looked carefully at the objects of your

worship, I found an altar on which was inscribed, "To an unknown god." What therefore you worship as unknown, this I proclaim to you.
(vv. 22–23)

It is here that Paul challenges the Athenians on their view of God:

The God who made the world and everything in it, being Lord of heaven and earth, does not live in shrines made by human hands. Nor is he served by human hands, as though he needed anything, since he himself gives to all life and breath and all things.
(vv. 24–25)

Paul chides these supposedly wise men for thinking lofty thoughts but worshiping lowly gods. Later, in verse 29, he insists, "We ought not to think that gold or silver or stone, fashioned by a craftsman and inscribed by a human, are like the Divine Being." God is the creator of all things; he sustains all things. No house can contain him, and no idol can properly represent him.

Squarely in the middle of this discussion of the one, true God's greatness, Paul adds a fascinating comment about God's intentions for humanity. Paul maintains that it was, in fact, *God* who had established the boundaries of the nations and allotted to humanity the places where people would live (v. 26).[2] Most importantly for our purposes, Paul says that "God did this . . . so they might *search for God* and so perhaps might *feel their way toward him* and find him, though he is not far from each one of us. For 'in him we live and move and have our being'; as even some of your own poets have said, 'For we too are his offspring'" (vv. 27–28).

Note the great contrast that results from this statement. On the one hand, we live and move and have our being *in God*. Yet, on the other hand, God wants us to *search* for him, to *feel our way* toward him, to *grope* for him. God is everywhere, and yet he must still be sought. This appears to be a key aspect of God's interaction with humanity. Part of the reason God remains elusive is because there is something fundamentally important about our *seeking* God. When God is not *sought*, our vision of God suffers as a result.

A Dangerous Temple

Paul's insistence that God "does not live in shrines made by human hands" (Acts 17:24) connects in an important way with the elusive nature of the tabernacle we saw in the previous chapter. As King David settles into his new palace, he is struck by the fact that *he* lives in an elaborate house of cedar "while the ark of God dwells in a tent" (2 Sam 7:2). But when the king proposes building the temple, a permanent house for God, the divine response is quite pointed: "Is it *you* who should build *me* a house to live in?" (v. 5). Speaking through the prophet Nathan, the divine message continues:

> I have not dwelt in a house from the day I brought up the Israelites from Egypt even to this day; *I move about in a tent and tabernacle*. In all my moving about among all the Israelites, have I ever spoken a word to any of the tribal leaders of Israel whom I commanded to shepherd my people Israel saying, "Why haven't you built me a house of cedar?"
> (vv. 6–7)

David was in danger in this moment of forgetting just who was the patron and who was the client in his relationship with God. David was not to think of himself as the one who would build a house (the temple) for God. On the contrary, God was the one who would build a house (a dynasty) for David (vv. 11–12).

At issue here was the fact that once God was thought to be tied down to a house, he would be, quite literally, *domesticated*. Our English word *domesticated* derives from a Latin word that means "belonging to the house." This is a meaning still found in phrases like *domestic life* or *domestic help*, both of which are tied to house and home. To domesticate something is to tame it, to curb its wilder instincts so it can be fit for service. Horses, cattle, and dogs, wheat, barley, and corn—all of these were once wild, but humans reined them in and set them to work on our behalf. The danger for our spiritual ancestors was in imagining that building a temple would do the same for God. It is only a small mental step from *building* a house for God to thinking one has *bound* God to that house. Solomon's prayer of dedication at the temple's completion sounded a note of warning concerning this very belief:

> Shall God truly dwell upon the earth? Behold, the heavens and the highest heavens cannot contain you, much less this house that I have built!
> (1 Kgs 8:27)

The sentiments in Solomon's prayer, however, appear to have gone largely unheeded. In time, many in Israel came to believe in the inviolability of Jerusalem, precisely because it was home to the temple. As the city of God and the location of the house of God, it was simply inconceivable that Zion could be conquered by any foreign foe. The very notion that the Lord's king, enthroned in the Lord's city of Zion, could be defeated was thought to elicit divine laughter (Ps 2:4–6). Unfortunately, this sort of thinking had disastrous results for the nation. Once they came to believe that they had tied God down in his temple, the people felt a certain liberty to drift from God in both their theological and their ethical commitments. Idolatry and immorality became rampant. And what was God going to do about it? It wasn't as if he could move his temple as he used to move his tabernacle.

The book of Ezekiel narrates the terrible end to which this sort of thinking finally led. While it might be true that God's house could never be defeated, if pushed, God would go so far as to abandon his house altogether. Ezekiel tells us that when God's anger over the idolatrous abominations that had come to fill the temple became too great (Ezek 8), God first removed his presence from the Holy of Holies to the temple threshold (9:3). From there, God's presence moved again to the east gate of the temple complex (10:19). Finally, it departed from Jerusalem entirely and headed east to the exiles in Babylon (11:23–25). Once God's presence had departed, the temple could no longer be thought of as God's house; Jerusalem could no longer be thought of as God's city. In short order, the Babylonians arrived and did what was once unthinkable: They destroyed them both.[3]

Though they wouldn't have put it in these terms, the Israelites had come to believe that with the construction of the temple, God was under a sort of "house arrest." At home in his temple, God was thought to need the ministrations of his servants as much as his servants needed him. Prophets like Jeremiah tried to warn the people that God would not be tied down in this manner. In his famous "Temple Sermon" in Jeremiah 7, the prophet warns the people, "Do not put your trust in deceptive words, saying 'The temple of the LORD, the temple of the LORD, the temple of the LORD!'" (v. 4). He tells them to look at what God had done to Shiloh. Though it had once been his home, the Shiloh shrine now stood in ruins because God had abandoned it (vv. 12–14). God would do the same to Jerusalem if the people didn't amend their ways (vv. 5–11). The God of Israel was an elusive God; he could not be pinned down, and he would not be contained.[4]

Misunderstood Sacrifices

Returning to Athens, we find that alongside Paul's observation that God "does not live in shrines made by human hands" is his insistence, "Nor is he served by human hands, as though he needed anything, since he himself gives to all life and breath and all things" (Acts 17:24–25). Just as it's a small mental step from building a house for God to imagining one has tied God down to that house, it's also a small step from serving God in the temple to thinking God is dependent upon his servants.

This was certainly the case among Israel's ancient neighbors. In the Mesopotamian story of the Flood, one of the results of the gods' wiping out humanity is that there were no more humans to provide the gods with sacrifices. Note the way the author describes the gods in Tablet XI of the Gilgamesh Epic when sacrifices are restored after the flood:

> The gods smelled the aroma.
> The gods smelled the sweet aroma.
> The gods gathered like flies around the man making the sacrifice.[5]

Israel wasn't immune to this same line of thinking. The indictment of the nation found in Psalm 50 rebukes the people for imagining that God was somehow dependent upon their sacrifices:

> It is not concerning your sacrifices that I rebuke you;
>   your burnt offerings are continually before me.
> I will not take a bull from your house,
>   nor a goat from your folds.
> For every animal of the forest is mine,
>   the cattle on a thousand hills.
> I know every bird of the mountains,
>   even the insects in the field are mine.
> If I were hungry, I would not tell you,
>   for the world and its fullness are mine.
> Do I eat the flesh of bulls
>   or drink the blood of goats?
>
>   (vv. 8–13)

The thought that God actually *needed* the people's sacrifices had a distorting effect on the nation's belief system. Many apparently understood their relationship with God to be transactional: God needed the sacrifices the nation provided, and so God was bound to provide blessings when those sacrifices were offered. Left to the side was the matter of obedience in the ethical realm and exclusivity of worship in the theological realm. Sacrifice in exchange for blessing was surely all that a God beholden to the sacrifices for sustenance could expect. Israel's prophets were at pains to argue that this was a terribly wrongheaded understanding of God and God's demands on the nation.

Nearly every prophet took the time to criticize the sacrificial system, not because sacrifices were thought to be wrong per se but because sacrifices left unmatched by ethical obedience were symptomatic of a fundamental misunderstanding of God. Thus, speaking through Amos, God insists:

> If you offer me burnt offerings and grain offerings,
>   I will not accept them.
> The peace offerings of your fatted animals
>   I will not look upon.
> Remove from my presence the noise of your songs;
>   I will not listen to the melody of your harps.
> But let justice roll down like waters
>   and righteousness like an ever-flowing stream.
>
>   (Amos 5:22–24)

Isaiah adds:

> "What to me is the multitude of your sacrifices?"
>   says the LORD.
> "I am sated with burnt offerings of rams
>   and the suet of fatted animals,
> The blood of bulls and sheep and goats
>   gives me no delight. . . .
> I cannot endure both iniquity and sacred assembly!"[6]
>
>   (Isa 1:11, 13b)

God didn't *need* the sacrifices that were offered to him, and when those sacrifices were offered without obedience in other areas, God rejected them:

> For you do not take delight in sacrifice;
>   if I were to give a burnt offering you would not take pleasure in it.
> God's sacrifices are a broken spirit;
>   a heart broken and crushed, O God, you would not despise.
>
>   (Ps 51:16–17)

> The sacrifice of the wicked is an abomination to the LORD;
>   but the prayer of the upright is his delight.
>
>   (Prov 15:8)

> Has the LORD as much delight in burnt offerings and sacrifices as in obeying the voice of the LORD?
>
> (1 Sam 15:22a)

The prophets, and others besides, recognized that Israel's sacrificial system didn't benefit God himself. If this system had value, it was for the nation and not for God. Believing otherwise, assuming that God actually needed the people's sacrifices, resulted in a distorted view of God. Ultimately, this bad theology took its toll on the spiritual health of the nation. God could not be domesticated and still be properly served at the same time.

A Necessary Search

Part of the answer to the question of why God is elusive is bound up in the *freedom* of God. God's elusiveness underscores for us the notion that he cannot be circumscribed, limited, or tied down. Just as importantly, though, *the elusiveness of God forces us to seek God to find him*. Put another way, the necessity of our seeking God helps us to properly understand who God is. The quest for God isn't a flaw in the divine economy; it's a feature. There is something vital about the search for God.

Testing That Produces Endurance

If we step outside the spiritual realm for a moment, most of us would recognize that a certain amount of struggle is vital to the human experience. In the movie *The Madness of King George*, viewers are invited to witness the difficult struggle of England's George III with the disease porphyria. Though the sitting monarch of one of the world's most powerful empires, King George descends into a kind of mania that renders him entirely incapable of ruling the country. Along the way, an unorthodox doctor, masterfully played by Ian Holm, is brought in to treat the mad king. The doctor's task is, of course, to help the king get back to normal. But what exactly would that be in the case of a king? In the doctor's words:

> Who's to say what's normal in a king? Deferred to, agreed with, acquiesced in. Who can flourish on such a daily diet of compliance? To be curbed, stood up to, in a word, thwarted, exercises the character, elasticates the spirit, makes it more pliant. It's the want of such exercise that makes rulers rigid.

In the absence of struggle, we fail to develop the toughness and resilience needed for life's many challenges.

Those of us who are parents know well the need to provide our children with moments of testing that will help them face the difficult world that awaits them. We give them chores to help them appreciate the value of hard work. We make them set money aside to learn the benefits of delayed gratification. We teach them to respect authority to prepare them to maneuver a world full of bosses and police officers and government officials and the like. The venues in which a similar dynamic is in place are too numerous to count. Football players go through "two-a-days" to develop the toughness needed for regular season. Baseball players slog through spring training for much the same reason. Dancers spend endless hours practicing their routines to be ready for the big night. Musicians drill their scales for hours to prepare for real pieces. Soldiers endure basic training to be ready for their eventual deployments. Students suffer through school—not in my classes, of course—to prepare themselves for a career. The book of Proverbs tells us that childhood itself is a sort of basic training for adult life (1:4; 3:1–2; 4:10; 13:1). The same sort of *necessary struggle* is also required for our spiritual life.

Necessary but Costly

When it comes to our relationship with God, there is something in the seeking that is just as vital as the finding. But though this may be true, we should not be naïve about what seeking God entails. Two things, in particular, will be true of our search:

First, our search for God is unlikely to end in anything approaching an encounter of biblical proportions. Many characters in the Bible meet God in powerful ways. Abraham hosts God and two of his angels at a meal prior to the destruction of Sodom and Gomorrah (Gen 18). Jacob wrestles with God (Gen 32). Moses encounters God at the burning bush (Exod 3–4). All of Israel witnesses God's approach at Sinai (Exod 19–24). Isaiah is caught up to see the very throne room of God (Isa 6). A host of characters—Joseph, Mary, Zechariah, the shepherds—receive angelic visitations in the story of Jesus' nativity (Matt 1–2; Luke 1–2). A handful of Jesus' disciples glimpse Christ's true self on the Mount of Transfiguration (Matt 17; Mark 9; Luke 9). Paul encounters Jesus on the road to Damascus (Acts 9). These are just a few of the many great theophanies narrated by the biblical authors. And, truthfully, we should not expect to duplicate a single one of them.

We'll return in a later chapter to the details of Jesus' appearance to Thomas a full week after he appeared to the other disciples. For now, it's enough to highlight just one line that Jesus says to Thomas when he finally comes to believe Jesus has risen from the dead. Standing before Thomas with pierced hands and wounded side ready for inspection, Jesus says, "You have believed because you have seen me; *blessed are those who have not seen and yet have believed*" (John 20:29). Jesus' words to Thomas tap into an important but often overlooked element of Scripture. While the Bible records many miracles and attests to many appearances of God or his emissaries, these were not the normal experiences of everyday Israelites. Most people within the pages of Scripture experienced life's ups and downs without ever seeing God's face or hearing his voice. They praised God when they were blessed and cried out to God when they suffered. They affirmed God's sovereignty on some occasions and mourned his absence on others. But they never actually saw God. Our aim in seeking God shouldn't be to stumble upon a second burning bush; our aim should be to join the ranks of those blessed by the Lord for believing even without those sorts of miracles.

Second, we should be clear-eyed in understanding that our search for God will not be without cost. Among the most familiar stories in the Gospels is that of Jesus' encounter with the so-called rich young ruler. As Matthew 19:16–21 recounts the story, a certain man asks Jesus, "Teacher, what good thing must I do to have eternal life?" Jesus replies:

> If you wish to enter life, keep the commandments. . . . You shall not murder; You shall not commit adultery; You shall not steal; You shall not bear false witness; Honor your father and mother; You shall love your neighbor as yourself.

Hearing this recitation of commands from the law, the young man replies, "All these I have kept; what do I still lack?" Jesus then says, "If you want to be complete, go sell whatever you have and give it to the poor, and you will have treasure in heaven; then, come follow me." Unfortunately, this was a bridge too far for the young man. Matthew tells us he was a man with many possessions, and so when he heard this word from Jesus, he slipped away, grieving as he went.

The story of the rich young ruler is not a story about wealth per se. Some who were wealthy followed Jesus; some who were poor did not. The real point of the story is not that following Jesus will cost us our fortunes; it's that it will cost us *everything*. If our search for God is like that of the psalmists, then we can expect nights of profound loneliness, questions that gnaw at us and won't go away, a spiritual and even physical fatigue that leaves us crying out as they did, "O Lord, how long!" It is almost enough to make us ask whether it's even worth it. I always seem to find the answer to that question in one particular interaction Jesus had with his disciples. John 6 describes a moment when the crowds following Jesus had increased, but apparently not for the right reasons. Jesus' response to this sudden burst of popularity was to delve into some very difficult matters in his teaching. As his words grew harder to understand or accept, the crowds slowly slipped away. In the end, only the Twelve were left. Seeing the disciples still gathered around him, Jesus asked, "Do you also want to leave?" It was Peter who replied with words that capture so many of our hearts: "Lord, to whom could we go? You are the one who has the words of eternal life" (vv. 67–68).

I am jealous of those who feel God's presence around them as readily as they feel the wind on a breezy day or sunshine in the summer. That hasn't been the experience of my spiritual journey. My soul bears the scars of a long and difficult search for God's presence, a search that has seen more pain than pleasure. The truth is, though, that I never really feel tempted to give up the search. Where else could I go? I remain convinced that Jesus still holds the words of life and that I will find them in the end.

How Do We Seek?

The Scriptures are clear in telling us that seeking is a vital part of our relationship with God. God is everywhere, but for us to understand him properly, for us to think of him rightly, we must still search for him. If this is the case, then the question for us is not one of *why* or *whether* but of *how*. How do we search for an elusive God?

In the chapters that follow, I offer what I hope will be a number of potential paths our search might take. Some fall into the category of what are often called the "spiritual disciplines"—study, silence, solitude, and the like. Others suggest a different road. Because we all start our spiritual journeys at different places, we all struggle with different obstacles. My hope is that whatever barriers we face in our own search for God's presence, some help along the way will be found here.

3

Seeking God in Scripture

My soul clings to the dust;
  revive me according to your word.
My soul melts away because of grief;
  sustain me according to your word.
    (Ps 119:25, 28)

The Road to Emmaus

ON A DAY LIKE NO OTHER, the very day of the resurrection, two of Jesus' disciples were walking from Jerusalem to the nearby town of Emmaus, discussing all the things that had happened on this first Easter weekend. While the disciples were rapt in conversation, a stranger came near and fell in with the men as they walked along. The stranger, it would turn out, was Jesus himself, but for the time being, his disciples' eyes were kept from perceiving the identity of their new traveling companion. Though he knew better than anyone else what events had transpired that day, Jesus still ventured to ask the disciples what they were going on about. Astonished that this stranger seemed unaware of the stories that had already begun to circulate, the two disciples began to relate the news of Jesus' death some three days earlier and of the empty tomb the women claimed to have found that very morning. The note of disappointment in their telling of the story was unmistakable. "We had hoped he was the one to redeem Israel," they said, but now their would-be Messiah was dead. And as for the astounding tales from the women about rolled-back stones, angelic visions, and an empty grave, well, who really knew what to believe?

A good storyteller would know that now was the time for the big "reveal." Surely, this was the moment Jesus would open the disciples' eyes and show them who he really was. But Jesus didn't do this at all. Instead, while his true identity remained hidden, he chastised the disciples for being so slow to understand what was truly going on. In the evangelist's words:

> Then he said to them, "O fools and slow of heart to believe all that the prophets have spoken! Was it not necessary for the Messiah to suffer these things and only then to enter into his glory?" *Then, beginning with Moses and with all the prophets, he explained to them in all the Scriptures the things concerning himself.*
> (Luke 24:25–27)

Jesus was physically present with the disciples, yet he felt it necessary to show them *from the Scriptures* what they should believe about him. It was only later, when the disciples convinced Jesus to stay the night with them, that the Messiah's true identity was revealed:

> And it happened when he reclined at dinner with them that he took bread and blessed it and broke it and gave it to them. Then their eyes were opened and they recognized him, but he vanished from their sight.
> (vv. 30–31)

The tension of "present yet elusive" could hardly be more evident in this passage. On the journey from Jerusalem to Emmaus, Jesus walked and talked with this pair of disciples; he was physically *present* with them. But at the same time, he prevented their eyes from recognizing who he truly was; he was *elusive* as well. Later, he reclined at dinner with them; once again, he was *present*. But when their eyes were opened and they recognized him, he vanished; once again, he was *elusive*. Not to be missed in the midst of this tension is the fact that though Jesus was there with the disciples, he still felt it necessary to show them *from the Scriptures* the truth about who he was. The disciples' own testimony affirms the method in Jesus' seeming madness. Luke tells us, "They said to each other, 'Did not our hearts burn within in us as he spoke to us on the way, as he opened up to us the Scriptures?'" (v. 32). It wasn't just the Messiah's physical presence that moved them; it was his opening up the Scriptures that pointed them even more clearly toward understanding. The path that led to an encounter with Jesus was a path that wound its way through the pages of Scripture.

The *Way* of Scripture

In retrospect, it may have been inevitable that the new messianic movement centered on a suffering figure like Jesus would be unable to find a home in the various strands of Second Temple Judaism. Whether inevitable or not, however, the "parting of the ways" between Judaism and Christianity that began in the decades after Pentecost only picked up steam in the centuries that followed. Others are surely better equipped to consider what Judaism may have lost as a result of this schism. For Christians, though, at least one lost element concerns the intense practicality of the Jewish approach to religion. As Christianity focused increasingly on what to *believe* in the Apostles' Creed, the Nicene Creed, and the Chalcedonian Creed, it paid somewhat less attention to the question of what to *do*. Orthopraxy lagged behind orthodoxy.

This matter of *doing* seems to be the nagging concern of James when he discusses the relationship of faith and works in his letter to the diaspora. As he reminds his readers of the need to live out their faith in works of charity, James insists, "You believe that God is one. You do well! Demons also believe this and shudder" (Jas 2:19). For James, demons aren't condemned because of any lack of orthodoxy in their beliefs about the nature of God. Their beliefs are fine; their actions are not. The same would be true of James' readers if their right beliefs were not lived out in right actions.

It's not that right beliefs are unimportant, of course; they most certainly are. And my theological commitments are such that I regard the Scriptures as the source and authority for defining those right beliefs. What is at stake here is rather a matter of rethinking how Scripture was meant to *function* in the life of the community. There is certainly a place for following in the footsteps of the Bereans who "searched the Scriptures daily" to see whether Paul's message was true (Acts 17:11). Too often, though, we seem to approach Scripture as a vast set of raw materials to be picked over for parts we can use to construct our systematic theologies and confessions of faith. The fact that the Scriptures are largely written in genres so ill-suited to this task ought to raise a hand of caution concerning this sort of theologically excavative reading. The Bible doesn't come to us as something akin to an Aristotelian philosophical reflection; it comes instead in the form of historical narratives, legal codes, prayers, and prophetic oracles. Even the more "systematically" theological portions of Scripture are generally letters sent to address particular issues in particular places at particular times. In Scripture, God hasn't given us a theological textbook; he has given us a *story* of his redemptive work—a story readers are invited to take part in as well. "Come, my children," the psalmist shouts. "Listen to me, and I will teach you the fear of the LORD" (Ps 34:11). Another says, "Come and see the deeds of God!" and "Come and hear, and I will tell all those who fear God what he has done for me" (Ps 66:5, 16). The psalmists' calls are from one pilgrim to another, urging fellow travelers onward in their divinely directed journey.

It is this sense of journey and movement that features so prominently in the biblical authors' descriptions of God's word. The familiar word *torah* is a noun derived from a verb meaning "to throw or cast." Its original sense appears to have been one of *pointing the way* or *pointing out a route*.[1] Not surprisingly, *torah*, whether referring to instruction generally or to *the* Torah, is often connected with verbs of motion. God's Torah is a *road* or *way* (*derek*) set before the people (Exod 18:20; Josh 22:5; 1 Kgs 2:3; 2 Chr 6:16; Isa 42:24). It is a *path* (*'ōraḥ*) to be followed (Isa 2:3; Mic 4:2). God's people should *walk* (*hālak*) in his Torah (Exod 16:4; 2 Kgs 10:31; 2 Chr 6:16; Neh 10:30; Ps 78:10; Jer 9:12; 26:14; 32:23; 44:10, 23; Dan 9:10). They are urged not to turn aside from it to the right or to the left (Josh 1:7; 23:6; Dan 9:11). So strong is this sense of motion associated with God's Torah that Judaism would come to use the term *halakha*, a noun derived from the Hebrew verb "to go" (*hālak*) and meaning essentially "the Way," to describe all of the various laws and statutes that guided daily living. It's interesting that the earliest Christians adopted similar terminology to describe their own new movement; in the book of Acts, Luke repeatedly describes Christianity as "the Way" (18:25, 26; 19:9, 23; 24:14, 22). The Greek term used here (*hē hodos*) is the same term the Septuagint (the ancient Greek translation of the Hebrew Bible) employs to translate the *road* or *way* found in God's Torah (as above, cf. Exod 18:20; Josh 22:5; 1 Kgs 2:3; 2 Chr 6:16; Isa 42:24).

The connection of God's word to a *way* of life is especially clear in the long Psalm 119. The psalmist begins his work by declaring, "O the happiness of those whose *way* is blameless, those who *walk* in the Torah of the LORD" (v. 1). Later, he adds, "The *way* of faithfulness I have chosen; your judgments I have set before me" (v. 30). He rejoices, "I *run* in the *way* of your commandments, for you broaden my understanding" (v. 32). Reflecting on God's word, he says, "A lamp to my *feet* is your word, a light to my *path*" (v. 105). By God's instructions, the psalmist says, "I *walk straight*; I hate every false *path*" (v. 128). Finally, he asks of God, "Keep *my steps* steady in your word; do not let any iniquity overpower me" (v. 133).

When two of Tolkien's beloved hobbits, Frodo and Samwise, set out on what will prove an exceedingly long journey from the Shire to Mordor and back again, their road out of the Shire reminds Frodo of something his Uncle Bilbo was wont to say:

> He used often to say there was only one Road; that it was like a great river: its springs were at every doorstep, and every path was its tributary. "It's a dangerous business, Frodo, going out of your door," he used to say. "You step into the Road, and if you don't keep your feet, there is no knowing where you might be swept off to."[2]

Though Bilbo warned his nephew about "the Road" that lay just outside his doorstep, it's clear he also found something irresistible about letting that same, dangerous road sweep him away. Scripture holds a similar attraction for us when we get past the matter of merely crossing confessional t's and dotting theological i's. When we allow ourselves to get caught up in the sweep of Scripture's riverine path, we slip into a current that ultimately promises to steer us back toward Scripture's Author.

Seeking God in Scripture

If the Way of Scripture offers a path for seekers in pursuit of an elusive God, then what exactly might it look like to take up that path?

Walk

In his extraordinary novel *East of Eden*, John Steinbeck weaves a tapestry of biblical allusions and echoes into his story of families struggling to make a go of it in the Salinas Valley in early twentieth-century California. Steinbeck's tale centers especially on a father, Adam, and his twin sons, Cal (for Caleb) and Aron (for Aaron). The names hearken back, of course, to Cain and Abel, as do the contours of their stories. Cal offers his father and brother profits from a somewhat unsavory agricultural sale, but his offering is rejected. In a fit of pique, Cal reveals a terrible family secret to his brother, Aron, who is so distraught that he enlists in the army and is soon killed in battle in World War I. Adam dies believing it was his favoritism toward Aron that drove Cal to lash out at his brother and send him to his death.

Over the course of the book, Steinbeck turns repeatedly to the story of Cain and Abel. It is Adam's Chinese housekeeper, Lee, who is particularly taken with God's word to Cain about the sin that "lieth at the door" (cf. Gen 4:7). "And unto thee shall be his desire," God says, "and *thou shalt* rule over him." "Thou shalt," Lee rightly observes, suggests a divine *promise* that Cain would overcome sin. But Cain did no such thing. Lee then consults another translation which has instead, "*Do thou* rule over him," a *command* instead of a promise. But which was the right interpretation? So concerned is Lee about the answer to this question that he travels to San Francisco to consult with the aged scholars who act as the patriarchs of his extended Chinese family. They, too, become wrapped up in the search for the phrase's true meaning, so much so that these nonagenarians take up the study of Hebrew to do so properly. Though these sages soon surpass the knowledge of the rabbi they had taken on to instruct them, two years of study pass before they feel confident enough to take up the Hebrew term in question, the verb *timshel*.[3] Long nights of debate and discussion follow, nights that finally bring them to an answer: *timshel* means neither "thou shalt" nor "do thou"; it means "*thou mayest*." It wasn't simply a promise that would inevitably be fulfilled. Nor was it a command that Cain had no ability to obey. "*Thou mayest* rule over it" set out a *choice* that Cain could fulfill but also might not. As Lee puts it:

> It is easy out of laziness, out of weakness, to throw oneself into the lap of deity, saying "I couldn't help it; the way was set." But think of the glory of the choice! That makes a man a man. A cat has no choice, a bee must make honey. There's no godliness there. And do you know, those old gentlemen who were sliding gently down to death are too interested to die now?[4]

It's this last line that casts such a fascinating image: a group of elderly Chinese scholars so captivated by the biblical text that they push off their appointment with death to keep studying it.

The Bible is a long and challenging book, but we won't make it any shorter or easier by trying to plow through it like end-of-semester reading for a college class. The ubiquitous "Read Through the Bible in a Year" plans call on the faithful to tackle three or four chapters of Scripture a day. When life intervenes, as it always does, those three or four chapters become six or eight or ten. Eventually, and understandably, most readers just give up. But even if we keep reading, how much Scripture works its way past our eyes and into our souls when we wolf it down in such large chunks? The great scholar of Israel's priestly literature, Jacob Milgrom, took nearly *four thousand* pages to explain the short twenty-seven chapters of Leviticus.[5] Can an average reader hope to penetrate the surface of this dense book by charging through four chapters of the book in a fifteen-minute sitting? We will seek God better in Scripture if we savor Scripture in the fashion of Steinbeck's elderly scholars rather than skim it like a stone skipping across a pond. When my students ask how they can grow in the Scriptures, I urge them to *walk* rather than run, to read *slowly* rather than quickly, to read one chapter a day rather than three. Or better yet, to read a single story or psalm one day, and then read it again and again for several days in a row. This is the sort of studying that slowly bores into one's soul.

Wander

Our first spiritual ancestors believed that the reading (and hearing) of Scripture played a central role in binding God's people to himself. It was this conviction that led the biblical authors to call so often for its *public* reading. At the conclusion of the covenant at Sinai, Moses "took the scroll of the covenant and read it in the hearing of the people" (Exod 24:7).[6] In the concluding chapters of Deuteronomy, we are told that as the people prepared to enter the promised land, "Moses spoke in the hearing of the whole congregation all the words of this Song to the very end" (Deut 31:30; cf. 32:44). Deuteronomy also orders that every seven years at the festival of Sukkoth (also known as Booths or Tabernacles), the whole of "this Torah" must be read aloud "before all Israel, in their hearing" (31:10–11).[7]

This tradition of the public reading of Scripture continued long after the Israelites had left the wilderness behind. When Joshua led the people into the promised land, he turned to the words of his predecessor, Moses:

> After this, *he read all the words of the Torah*, the blessing and the curse, just as everything was written on the scroll of the Torah. There was not a word from all that Moses had commanded them that Joshua did not read before the whole congregation of Israel, with the women and the children and the sojourners that were in their midst.
>
> (Josh 8:34–35)

When the "scroll of the Torah" was found in Josiah's time, the king insisted that it be read publicly:

> The king went up to the house of the Lord, with every man of Judah and all the inhabitants of Jerusalem, along with the priests and the prophets and all the people, from the least to the greatest. *And he read in their hearing* all the words of the scroll of the covenant that had been found in the house of the Lord.
> (2 Kgs 23:2; cf. 2 Chr 34:30)

When the exiles returned from captivity in Babylon, it was the public reading of Scripture that ultimately bound them together:

> Ezra opened the scroll in the sight of the people, for he stationed himself above the people, and when he opened it, all the people stood. And Ezra blessed the Lord the Great God, and all the people answered, "Amen, amen!" with their hands upraised. They bowed and prostrated themselves before the Lord with their faces on the ground. . . . The Levites explained the Torah to the people while the people were standing. *They read from the scroll of the Torah of God*, interpreting it and giving the sense of it, so that the people understood the reading.
> (Neh 8:5–8)

Even in the New Testament, Paul exhorts his disciple Timothy: "Until I arrive, give attention to *reading*, to exhortation, to teaching" (1 Tim 4:13). The particular term used here for "reading," *anagnōsis*, is elsewhere used in the New Testament only for the public reading of Scripture (cf. Acts 13:15; 2 Cor 3:14).

Biblical authors called for the reading of Scripture so often because they were convinced that God's word was uniquely invested with the power to shape God's people. Thus, for example, the prophet assures us in Isaiah that God's word always accomplishes his purpose:

> For just as the rain and snow come down from the heavens and do not return there without watering the earth and causing it to bring forth and sprout and produce seed for planting and bread to eat, so it is with my Word, which goes forth from my mouth and *does not return to me empty, but rather accomplishes what I desire and succeeds in what I sent it to do.*
> (Isa 55:10–11)

This word of assurance in Isaiah is set in the context of the seemingly inscrutable nature of God's workings. His plans are not our plans, we are told

(v. 9); God works to accomplish his will in ways only the patient can perceive. In the same way, the effect of Scripture on us is not always perfectly straightforward. Scripture can affect us in the same way that music or art affects us. We can't always put our finger on some objective truth we have learned from this passage or that, and yet God's word slowly and subtly shapes us through our interaction with it.

When the author of Psalm 1 describes the manifold "happinesses" (the Hebrew *'ašrēy* is plural!) of the righteous person, he ties that person's happiness to the fact that they "meditate" on the Lord's Torah (v. 2). The Hebrew term used here for *meditate* is *hāgâ*, a word whose range of meanings extends from the cooing of a dove (Isa 38:14; 59:11) to the growling of a lion (Isa 31:4) to the rumbling that comes from one's throat (Job 37:2; Ps 115:7) and even to the sigh of those who see their years come to an end (Ps 90:9). What ties these uses together is their sense of a sound that comes from deep within. The righteous find happiness because they have so deeply internalized God's word that it bubbles up from the depths of their soul when the moment is right. This sort of deep internalization doesn't come from blithely skipping through (and over) the biblical text. It comes from the same sort of slow meandering and savoring that fits a leisurely drive in the country, not a hurried commute on the interstate.

A favorite student of mine once told me she had recently been immersing herself in Scripture in a way she never had before. She confessed that it was having an effect on her she could hardly explain. It wasn't that she was learning lots of facts or discerning new theological niceties. "It's just changing me," she said. This is the effect of Scripture one psalmist identifies when he says, "I store up your word in my heart, so I might not sin against you" (Ps 119:11). Another says, "The Torah of his God is in his heart, so that his feet do not slip" (Ps 37:31). In still another place, God tells Joshua, "Do not let the scroll of this Torah depart from your mouth; meditate on it day and night so you may be careful to do all that is written in it" (Josh 1:8). These passages add to the observation of my student the notion that as we drink from God's word, it courses through us and affects the entirety of our being. We are changed from the inside out as we wander through Scripture and let it slowly rewire our instincts.

Wrestle

As we seek after God by walking and wandering through the pages of Scripture, we shouldn't imagine that the path will always be an easy one. Steep hills, narrow passes, and rocky stretches await those who read and *read carefully* the Scriptures. How can we *not* struggle when we read God's command to Abraham to sacrifice his beloved son, Isaac? It is all well and good to argue that God never really intended for Abraham to kill his son, that this was God's way of showing he did not desire human sacrifice, or that this would illustrate the terrible sacrifice at the cross in centuries to come. I'm largely persuaded by all of these ideas. But how can we linger over this text without wrestling with those fateful words: "Take your son, your only son, whom you love, Isaac, and go to the land of Moriah and offer him there as a burnt offering" (Gen 22:2)? Is there no moment of pause in our hearts when we read about the terrible sufferings of Job and find that their source lay in what seems to be a wager between God and Satan (Job 1:6–12; 2:1–7)? Is there no sense of confusion, no sense of injustice even at the seemingly trivial cause of Moses' exclusion from the promised land (Num 20:11)? To return to a passage noted above, do we not feel at least a modicum of sympathy for Cain whose offering was rejected for reasons he couldn't begin to fathom (Gen 4:5)?

I realize that raising these sorts of issues is apt to create confusion (or stronger feelings still) among some readers. I would argue, however, that wrestling with these sorts of passages places us in a long line of readers *within the Bible itself*. Cain cried out, "My punishment is greater than I can bear!" (Gen 4:13). Abraham questioned God's justice when God proposed to destroy Sodom and Gomorrah (Gen 18:25). Moses begged God to reverse his sentence of banishment from the promised land (Deut 3:24–25). Throughout Scripture, a host of characters cry out to God with words of lament, asking God why he has acted in one way or another.

Our spiritual ancestors recognized the challenges Scripture poses to its readers. Few authors in the Bible receive more attention than the apostle Paul, yet the concluding verses of 2 Peter admit concerning Paul's letters: "There are in them *some things that are hard to understand*, which the ignorant and unstable distort to their own destruction" (3:15–16). Even passages less challenging than Paul's letters can require assistance to understand. When Ezra and the Levites read the Torah to the assembled Jews in Jerusalem, the text tells us, "They read from the scroll of the Torah of God *explaining and giving the sense of it so that they understood the reading*" (Neh 8:8). Ezra, and a succession of interpreters since, recognized that interpretation and explanation are often necessary to understand God's word. To return to our earlier story of the road to Emmaus, even the disciples needed the risen Lord to "interpret to them the things about himself in all the Scriptures, beginning with Moses and all the prophets" (Luke 24:27).

Venturing back to a passage mentioned in the previous chapter, Jesus' interaction with the crowds and his disciples in John 6 vividly illustrates how wrestling with God's word is a vital part of a life of faith. In this key text, Jesus seems dissatisfied with the fact that so many had begun to follow him solely because he miraculously provided them with fish and loaves to eat (v. 26). Seemingly as a way of separating casual followers from the committed, he challenges his hearers with the message that he is the bread of life and those who want eternal life must eat his flesh and drink his blood (vv. 48–58). At this, even Jesus' disciples admit to the difficulty of his teaching. "This is a hard saying," they lament. "Who can bear to hear it?" (v. 60). Jesus doesn't shy away from the provocative nature of his message; quite the contrary, he acknowledges that what he has to say is so hard that it is only by the Father's drawing that a person could come to him (v. 65). When Jesus then asks the disciples if they also want to leave, Peter responds, "To whom could we go? Only you have the words of eternal life" (v. 68). Peter's answer was not a denial of the difficulty of Jesus' teaching; it was an admission of it. But Peter also recognized that however hard Jesus' words might be, *the truth could not be found anywhere else.*

4

Seeking God in Nature

How many are your works, O Lord!
  Through wisdom you have made them all;
  the earth is full of your creations.
    (Ps 104:24)

Caught Off Guard

THERE ARE MOMENTS, UNEXPECTED MOMENTS, when creation sneaks up on you, slips quietly from a hidden corner, leaps out, and simply takes your breath away.

There was the time I was driving alongside the Hudson River just north of New York City, passing through the tiny hamlets of West Haverstraw, Tomkins Cove, and Jones Point. It was just a relaxing drive in the fall, and then there appeared the most glorious, autumn-bedecked tree I have ever seen. The leaves of the tree had been transformed to hues of yellow and orange so vivid that they seemed to have been set ablaze by the afternoon sun. They burned with the intensity of a bonfire against the backdrop of a cobalt blue sky. Unexpected. Out of nowhere. Overwhelming. In that moment, creation itself seemed alive with beauty.

There was that time at Snow Creek Falls on the north rim of the Yosemite Valley. The work of setting up camp could wait a while longer as we rushed to the cliff's edge to see the sunset on Half Dome. A riot of colors jostled for attention against that perfect granite canvas. We traced the rising shadow and disappearing light as the sun slowly sank beyond the horizon, wishing it would hold off just a little longer. In that moment, it was as though God had etched his autograph in light and stone for all to see.

There was that drive through the Avenue of the Giants in Northern California. It took every ounce of concentration I could muster to stay focused on the road as one impossibly large redwood after another gripped the earth with its roots and reached toward the heavens with its canopy. These were somber, silent giants standing at attention, seemingly oblivious to tiny figures like us scurrying about at their feet. As we walked among those wooden pillars of creation, it felt as if we stumbled upon a garden God had planted just for himself.

There was that time during a particular class in grad school when snow began to fall outside our windows. By the time class was over, the grass had disappeared under a soft blanket of white. Standing at the top of a long stairway, looking over the rest of campus below and the hilly western suburbs of Boston in the distance, a dear friend who had been trying so hard to be an atheist let slip, "There just has to be a God." As those feathery snowflakes drifted toward the ground, it was as if whispers of God's divinity swirled all around us.

A God Evident in Nature

Scripture is our surest guide to understanding who God is and what God expects of us. When we immerse ourselves in the pages of Scripture, we slip into a stream whose currents work to carry us along toward its Author. But Scripture itself attests to the fact that God has revealed himself not just in his word but also in his creation.

With a bit of searching, visitors to London's St. Paul's Cathedral can locate a plaque inscribed with a brief Latin dedication: *Si monumentum requiris circumspice*, "If a monument you seek, look around." This inscription is dedicated to Sir Christopher Wren, the architect who designed the cathedral and oversaw its construction. While the lives of other notable figures are commemorated with imposing statues or elaborate tombs, the great cathedral itself serves as Wren's monument. What is true of Sir Christopher's cathedral is infinitely more true of God's creation.

The Scriptures are quick to tell us that God "does not dwell in houses made by human hands" (Acts 7:48). Certainly, no cathedral or temple could circumscribe him. As Solomon exclaims at the dedication of his own famous temple, "Behold, the heavens and the highest heavens cannot contain you, much less this house that I have built!" (1 Kgs 8:27). In Isaiah, the Lord insists, "The heavens are my throne, and the earth a footstool for my feet" (Isa 66:1). But if even the entirety of creation is insufficient to contain an infinite God, Scripture insists that nature nevertheless stands as a witness to God's existence and his mighty power.

Creation and the Grandeur of God

Biblical authors appeal constantly to nature as an expression of the grandeur of God. The first half of Psalm 19 does so in memorable fashion:

> The heavens declare the glory of God,
>   and the firmament proclaims the work of his hand.
> One day gushes forth speech to another day,
>   and one night declares knowledge to another night.
> There is no speech, and there are no words;
>   their voice is not heard.
> And yet their voice[1] goes out through all the earth,
>   their words to the ends of the world!
>
>   (Ps 19:1–4a)

In the psalmist's reckoning, the heavens above take on the role of heralds who announce to one and all the greatness of the God who created them. The psalmist personifies day and night as messengers who return with reports concerning God's glory and pass their messages along to the next day and night as they begin their terms of service. Of particular note is the way the psalmist describes the manner of creation's heralds. In one sense, the heavens, the firmament, and even day and night are silent; there is no actual speech to be heard from them, no words or voice. But in another sense, the voice of these marvels of creation booms from one end of the world to the other.[2]

The poet who composed Psalm 8 begins and ends his song with a shout of praise grounded in the way creation reflects the majesty of its Creator:

> O Lord, our Lord, how mighty is your name in all the earth,
>   you who have set your majesty above the heavens!
>
>   (vv. 1, 9)

The psalmist's use of the phrase "mighty is your *name*" is particularly important. The biblical notion of "name" (*šēm*) often has less to do with one's title than with one's *reputation* and even *fame*. In the language of Proverbs 22:1, "A *name* is to be chosen over great riches." Ecclesiastes 7:1 adds, "Better is a *name* than fine oil."[3] In Psalm 8, it is creation itself that reveals and proclaims God's reputation. The more majestic the creation, the more exalted is God's name. But it is this sheer majesty in creation (and thus in God) that poses such a dilemma for the psalmist: How could a God who created the heavens, the moon, and the stars pay any notice at all to human beings?

> When I see your heavens, the work of your fingers,
>   the moon and the stars that you established,
> what are humans that you remember them,
>   mortals that you pay attention to them?
>
> (vv. 3–4)

The words used by the psalmist to describe humanity, *ĕnôš* and *ben-'āḏām*, emphasize the distance between God and mortal humans. On a purely linguistic level, the former term appears to be connected to the Semitic nominal root *'nš*, signifying merely "human." On various occasions, though, a wordplay with the verbal root consisting of the same consonants appears to be intended. This *'nš* refers, significantly, to "being weak" and underscores the frailty of humanity; it is this hinted-at frailty that marks such a contrast with the God of all creation.[4] The latter term, *ben-'āḏām*, appears most often in the book of Ezekiel (ninety-four times!) as a means of underscoring the *mortality* of the prophet. As great as the heavens may be, their Creator must be greater still. But how could a God so great be mindful of mortals so small?

The psalmists are not alone in their conviction that nature has a place in revealing the presence and power of God. In his letter to the Romans, the apostle Paul finds in creation sufficient revelation of God's nature to condemn those who exchange true worship for idolatry:

> For that which is known about God is evident to them, because God made it evident to them. For his invisible attributes, his eternal nature, power, and divinity, have been understood and seen from the creation of the world *in what has been made*, so that they are without excuse.
>
> (Rom 1:19–20)

The book of Acts preserves a similar message as it recalls an occasion when an admiring crowd of Gentiles takes Barnabas and Paul to be Zeus and

Hermes come to earth in human form (cf. 14:8–18). The two evangelists desperately urge the crowd not to offer sacrifices to them, demanding, "Men, why are you doing this? We are human beings with the same passions as you!" (v. 15a). They quickly direct the crowd's devotion elsewhere:

> Turn from these worthless things to the living God who made the heavens and the earth and the sea and all that is in them. In past generations, he permitted the nations to walk in their own ways, yet *he did not leave himself without a witness* of doing good—giving you rain from heaven and fruitful seasons, satisfying your hearts with food and cheer.
> (vv. 15b–17)

Note that Barnabas and Paul find in creation evidence of God's true nature and goodness. Even when God's written revelation had not yet been shared with the nations outside of Israel, Paul says that God had "left a witness" in the form of nature to point the nations to him.

Creation and the Futility of Idols

It is this "witness" of creation that presses the Israelite prophets to rail against the worship of idols with such particular force. Isaiah 44 roundly mocks the notion that human artisans could fashion their own deities:

> He plants a laurel tree, and the rain makes it grow. Then one can burn it. He takes some of it and uses it to warm himself. He kindles a fire with it and bakes bread; then he fashions a god from it and worships it. He makes it into an idol and bows down to it. Half of it he burns in the fire; on that half is meat that he eats. He roasts the meat and is satisfied. He also warms himself and says, "Ah, I am warm! I see the firelight!" Then the rest of it he makes into a god, an idol for himself. He bows down to it, worships it, and prays to it. He says, "Save me, for you are my god!"
> (vv. 14b–17)

What sort of god, the prophet demands, could be fashioned from a log that is just as suitable for firewood as it is for an idol? Jeremiah joins in with similar words of derision:

> The customs of the peoples are worthless. For it is a tree that one cut down from the forest, the work of the hands of a craftsman with a tool.

He decorates it with silver and gold. With nails and hammers, he secures it so that it won't totter. They are like scarecrows in a cucumber field. They cannot speak. They must be carried because they cannot walk. Have no fear of them, for they cannot do evil, nor is it in them to do good!
(Jer 10:3–5)

Even the psalmists take their turn at ridiculing these so-called gods:

Their idols are silver and gold,
    the work of human hands.
Mouths they have, but they cannot speak;
    eyes they have, but they cannot see.
Ears they have, but they cannot hear;
    noses they have, but they cannot smell.
Hands, but they cannot touch;
    feet but they cannot walk;
nor can they make a sound with their throats.
(Ps 115:4–7)

Almost without exception, when the biblical authors inveigh against the worship of idols, they invoke the image of God as Creator to bolster their attacks. So-called gods formed by human hands pale in comparison to the God whose hands made heaven and earth. The same passage in Isaiah 44 that ridicules the woodsman's firewood idol extols God the Creator:

Thus says the LORD, your Redeemer,
    who formed you in the womb,
I am the LORD who made all things,
    who alone stretched out the heavens,
    who spread out the earth by myself.
(v. 24)

In the same text where he mocks idols as "scarecrows in a cucumber patch," Jeremiah exclaims:

Let the gods *who did not make the heavens and the earth* perish from the earth and from under the heavens. *He made the earth* by his power; *he established the world* by his wisdom; and by his understanding, *he stretched out the heavens.*
(Jer 10:11–12)[5]

The psalmist who chides the nations' idols as mute, blind, and deaf prays, "May you be blessed by the Lord, *maker of heaven and earth*" (Ps 115:15).

There is something remarkable in the Israelites' attacks on idolatry and, for that matter, in their attacks on polytheism generally. Gods and their images were ubiquitous in the ancient world. Idols ranging from portable trinkets to monumental stone statues were part and parcel of the worship of every nation the Israelites encountered. Jacob's Aramean father-in-law, Laban, seemed as worried about the loss of his household gods as he did about the loss of his two daughters when his son-in-law fled back toward Canaan (Gen 31:19–35). The Philistines rushed to send the ark of the covenant back to Israel when it inflicted damage on their idol-god Dagon (1 Sam 5). The Babylonians were convinced that the fall and later restoration of their empire were directly linked to the loss of an idol of their god Marduk. The supposedly enlightened Greeks were taken to task by Paul for their many idols (Acts 17:16, 31). Yet, in the midst of this seeming unanimity of belief concerning the gods and their images, the Israelite prophets stood up and declared, in effect, "The emperor has no clothes!" *God made the universe; humans cannot make gods.*

For the prophets, it was self-evident that creation declares the existence and character of its Creator. Creation serves as a sort of divine provocation, forcing humanity to acknowledge God's power (through creation's grandeur) and God's goodness (through creation's bounty). It is in this provocative sense that creation serves as the witness marked by Paul and Barnabas. Elsewhere in the book of Acts, witnesses are almost always those called upon to *challenge* hearers with the message of Christ's resurrection (Acts 1:8; 2:32; 3:15; 5:32; 10:39–41; 13:31; 22:15, 20; 23:11). Witnesses are not merely bystanders available to testify when needed. They are provocateurs, laying out their evidence whether their hearers care to listen or not. So it is with creation. It declares, proclaims, confronts, and challenges. It demands a response.

Seeking God in Nature

If creation declares the glory of God, then it stands to reason that this same creation offers seekers an additional path alongside Scripture to find our way back to God. The question, then, is just how we can do this.

Get Back to Nature

We live in worlds too often closed off from nature. If God reveals himself in creation, then a life cut off from the natural world is one necessarily cut off from this aspect of God's self-communication. But cut off we certainly are.

I have a fireplace in my house but truthfully I burn wood in it not to heat my home but for the aesthetic effect it provides. Sunlight reaches the interior of my home, but only as I allow it to through energy-efficient windows and a phalanx of curtains and blinds adjusted to my taste. My thermostat keeps the temperature pleasantly cool in summer and comfortably warm in winter. When I want water, no pumping is involved, much less hauling a bucket from a spring; I merely turn the handle on a faucet. Meat comes antiseptically wrapped in cellophane. Vegetables are conveniently stored in cans or frozen in bags made of plastic. Bread comes not from the sweat of my brow but from a swipe of my credit card. I live in a bubble, enjoying the fruits of nature but cut off from nature itself. And in this regard, I'm certainly not alone.

It's not hard to understand why the English Romantics rebelled against the growing alienation of humanity from nature that accompanied the Industrial Revolution. As Wordsworth observed in his poem "The World Is Too Much with Us," something was lost in one area as something was gained in another:

> The world is too much with us; late and soon,
> Getting and spending, we lay waste our powers;—
> Little we see in Nature that is ours;
> We have given our hearts away, a sordid boon!

This same feeling of loss is evident in the poet's protest against the extension of railway service into England's picturesque Lake District. In "On the Projected Kendal and Windermere Railway," Wordsworth laments:

> Is then no nook of English ground secure
> From rash assault? Schemes of retirement sown
> In youth, and 'mid the busy world kept pure
> As when their earliest flowers of hope were blown,
> Must perish; how can they this blight endure?

Those familiar with Tolkien's work will recognize similar sentiments in his narration of the hobbits' return to their beloved but now badly mistreated Shire:

> It was one of the saddest hours in their lives. .... As they crossed the bridge and looked up the Hill they gasped. Even Sam's vision in the Mirror had not prepared him for what they saw. The Old Grange on the west side had been knocked down, and its place taken by rows of tarred sheds. All the chestnuts were gone. The banks and hedgerows were broken. Great waggons were standing in disorder in a field beaten bare of grass. Bagshot Row was a yawning sand and gravel quarry. Bag End up beyond could not be seen for a clutter of large huts.[6]

Tolkien's harrowing experiences in the First World War find echoes in his many descriptions of battle and war in Middle-earth. But the near loss of the Shire strikes an even deeper chord of sorrow. The tears Sam sheds when he sees Bilbo's Party Tree "lying lopped and dead in the field" are surely the author's own tears over England's rapid loss of countryside to industry.

We don't need to agree with every line of the Romantic catechism to admit the element of truth in these feelings of loss and alienation. There is no need to overly idealize Nature as Wordsworth did in "Lines Composed a Few Miles above Tintern Abbey" when he claimed:

> My dear, dear Sister! and this prayer I make,
> Knowing that Nature never did betray
> The heart that loved her; 'tis her privilege,
> Through all the years of this our life, to lead
> From joy to joy.

Nor do we need to imagine with Shelley in his poem "Mont Blanc" that Nature could speak truth that would dispel the supposed falsehoods ("large codes of fraud") of organized religion:

> The wilderness has a mysterious tongue
> Which teaches awful doubt, or faith so mild,
> So solemn, so serene, that man may be,
> But for such faith, with Nature reconcil'd;
> Thou hast a voice, great Mountain, to repeal
> Large codes of fraud and woe; not understood
> By all, but which the wise, and great, and good
> Interpret, or make felt, or deeply feel.

Rousseau was naive to imagine he would find Eden in the more "primitive" environs of Tahiti, and Gauguin seemed to admit as much when he attempted suicide after painting such a bleak portrayal of Tahiti's so-called paradise in "D'où venons-nous? Que sommes-nous? Où allons-nous?" ("Where do we come from? What are we? Where are we going?"). But the fact that the Romantics failed in their search for a cure doesn't mean they had also failed in diagnosing a growing ailment in the human condition.

Much of the Bible looks with a skeptical eye on cities and the sort of "civilization" they offer. In the early chapters of Genesis, for example, it is surely a matter of some significance that humanity's first city-builder is the banished murderer Cain (Gen 4:17). A bit later in the book, in the so-called Tower of Babel story in Genesis 11, it isn't the tower that's at issue but *the city*. The gathered multitudes attempt to build "*a city* and a tower" (v. 4). God comes down to see "*the city* and the tower" (v. 5). And when God thwarts the people's efforts by confusing their tongues, we're told, "They stopped building *the city*"; the tower is left unmentioned (v. 8). A few chapters later, it is the "cities of the plain" that beguile Abraham's nephew, Lot, luring him in their direction as he pitches his tent near the city of Sodom (Gen 13:12). It won't be long before Lot and his family are swallowed up entirely by city life—so much so that even as the city is being destroyed, they resist the angelic warnings to leave. In the end, the angels must seize Lot and his family by the hand and drag them outside the city (Gen 19:16); and even then, their efforts are only half successful. Lot's wife famously turns back to the city, and Lot himself begs the divine messengers to let him flee to another city nearby (v. 20).

Scripture would tell us we are more suited to the natural setting of a garden than the walled confines of a city. The Bible's earliest creation traditions insist that God made us to live in a garden: "The LORD God planted a garden in Eden, and he placed the man he had created there, . . . and the LORD God took the man, and he placed him in the Garden of Eden to work it and take care of it" (Gen 2:8, 15). It was in a garden that the man and the woman first experienced the presence of God, and it was from that garden presence that the curse banished the first couple:

> The LORD God cast them out of the Garden of Eden to work the ground from which they had been taken. He drove the man out, and he stationed east of the Garden of Eden the cherubim and a flaming sword, constantly turning to guard the way to the Tree of Life.
> (Gen 3:23–24)

It is a return to this garden that the prophets long for in their visions of the age to come. The prophet announces in Isaiah 51:3a, "For the LORD has comforted Zion, comforted all of her ruins. He has made her wilderness *like Eden* and her desert *like the Garden of the Lord.*" Ezekiel expresses similar sentiments when he declares:

> Thus says, the Lord YHWH, "On the day when I have cleansed you from all your iniquities, I will cause your cities to be resettled and your ruins to be rebuilt. I will cause that desolate land to be worked again; no longer shall it lie desolate in the eyes of every one who passes by. They will say, '*That desolate land has become like the Garden of Eden*, and the cities and the ruins that were desolate and ruined are fortified once more.'"
>
> (Ezek 36:33–35)

Even the holy city of Jerusalem is cast in terms befitting a garden in Revelation's vision of the world to come:

> He showed me a river of living water, clear as crystal, flowing from the throne of God and the Lamb in the middle of its street. On either side of the river was the tree of life, producing twelve fruits, yielding its fruit each month, and the leaves of the tree were for healing the nations.
>
> (Rev 22:1–2)

The roots of our family tree were first planted in a garden, and the full flourishing of that tree's boughs will take place in a garden again. In the meantime, as we make our way from that first garden to the last, we can find signs of God's presence in the natural world of which these gardens were a part.

Cultivate a Sense of Wonder

It's fair to say that John Muir was an idiosyncratic sort of Christian. He was perhaps too enamored with transcendentalists like Thoreau and Emerson (American versions, roughly, of the English Romantics) and too little appreciative of the fact that creation is both beautiful *and broken*. The eccentricities that compelled Muir to set out alone into the wilds of Yosemite with little more than a blanket and some hardtack were bound to manifest themselves in his theology as well. Truthfully, it is well nigh a miracle that Muir remained a Christian of any sort given the overly stern upbringing he experienced at the hand of his father. A great chasm lies between the sentiment, "Thy Word have I hid in mine heart that I might not sin against Thee," and forcing the memorization of Scripture upon a young man at the end of a lash. Efforts to hammer Scripture into Muir could have just as easily served to drive Christianity out of him instead.[27] And yet, remain a believer Muir certainly did. Even a cursory glance at his writings reveals Muir's profound Christian faith. Consider, for example, the close of this letter written in 1900 to comfort a friend whose sister had died:

> Read again and again those blessed words, ever old, ever new: "Who redeemeth thy life from destruction; who crowneth thee with loving kindness and tender mercy," who pities you "like as a father pitieth his children, for He knoweth our frame, He knoweth that we are dust. Man's days are as grass, as a flower of the field the wind passeth over it and it is gone, but the mercy of the Lord is from everlasting to everlasting." In His strength we must live on, work on, doing the good that comes to heart and hand, looking forward to meeting in that City which the streams of the River of Life make glad.[7]

These are not the words of a pantheist or pagan.

However grievous the manner of their acquisition, the words of Scripture hidden in John Muir's heart found a happy union with the naturalist's love for God's creation. Note the prayerlike quality of his description of a night in the Sierra Nevada mountains:

> The place seemed holy, where one might hope to see God. After dark, when the camp was at rest, I groped my way back to the altar boulder and passed the night on it,—above the water, beneath the leaves and stars,—everything still more impressive than by day, the fall seen dimly white, singing Nature's old love song with solemn enthusiasm, while the stars peering through the leaf-roof seemed to join in the white water's song. Precious night, precious day to abide in me forever. Thanks be to God for this immortal gift.[8]

Muir worked tirelessly to persuade the politicians of his day to protect America's natural wonders. But he was just as indefatigable in his attempts to persuade ordinary citizens of the beauty and wonder of nature. He grew impatient with those so caught up in the pursuit of commerce that they refused to look up and see the beauty of the natural world around them:

> They cannot pause long enough to go out into the wilderness where God has provided every sparrow enough to eat and to spare, and contemplate for even an hour the wonderful world that they live in.[9]

As a counterexample to this obsession with the sort of "bigger barns" Jesus derided in his parables (cf. Luke 12:18), Muir's writings model an embrace of the simplicity and beauty of the natural world. Even a short journal entry on an unnamed stretch of forest exudes a spirit of wonder at the majesty of creation and a spirit of reverence for its Creator:

> The air is distinctly fragrant with balsam and resin and mint—every breath of it a gift we may well thank God for. . . . God himself seems to be always doing his best here, working like a man in a glow of enthusiasm.[10]

Those seeking God's presence could do worse than to heed Muir's call to drink deeply from the refreshing streams of God's creation, to rekindle the sense of wonder we possessed so naturally as children. Not so long ago, there seemed to be no end to our fascination with twinkling stars and flittering butterflies and leaves as they fell from autumn trees. But with adulthood, we come to resemble nothing so much as the thorny soil that lets "the cares of the world and the lure of wealth" choke creation's sermon of praise for its Creator (cf. Matt 13:22).

Remember That Bounty Is a Blessing

While our liturgical calendar is filled with holy days and sacred feasts, Christianity has largely abandoned the inheritance of festivals passed down by the ancient Israelites. Christians may have holidays to spare, but it's still the case that something important was lost in setting aside these Old Testament observances. Most obvious, of course, is the erosion of the Hebrew foundations for holidays like Easter and Pentecost. The depths of meaning in the Last Supper and Christ's great deliverance at the cross cannot be fully plumbed apart from the Israelite Passover. Less obvious, but perhaps more consequential, in Christianity's disregard for the First Testament's festivals has been the loss of a uniquely Israelite genius concerning sacred moments.

Israel's annual festivals stand out for the way they wed the events of salvation history with the events of the agricultural cycle. The festivals of Passover and Unleavened Bread are naturally concerned with God's deliverance of his people from Egypt, but they were also connected with the spring lambing season (in the case of Passover) and the beginning of the spring barley harvest (in the case of Unleavened Bread). The festival of Shavuot or "Weeks" came to commemorate the giving of the Torah at Sinai, but it was also connected with the end of the barley harvest.[11] The fall festival of

Sukkoth served to recall the temporary shelters (tents) in which the Israelites dwelled during their wilderness wanderings, but its origins lay in the temporary shelters workers would build when they needed to sleep in their fields during harvest time.

By linking great moments of divine deliverance to key events in the agricultural year, Israel forged a link between bounty and blessing. Seedtime and harvest were not just part of the hard work of farming; they were moments for remembering that God had delivered the nation in the past and that he continued to bless the nation in the present. No text captures this link between salvation and blessing more clearly than Deuteronomy 26. In this early creedal formula, Moses commands the Israelites to take a portion of the firstfruits from their harvest, place it in a basket, and bring it to the altar. There, in the presence of the priests, they are to recount the story of God's deliverance of Israel. "A wandering Aramean was my father," they are to recall, and from there they are to remember the steps that took Israel down to Egypt and back up from suffering and slavery. Then come the key lines of this early catechism:

> He brought us to this place, and he gave us this land, a land flowing with milk and honey, and so now I have brought the first of the fruits of the ground that you gave me, O Lord!
> (vv. 9–10)

In this confession and the accompanying offering of firstfruits, we find clear recognition of the fact that the bounty we enjoy is part of an endless chain of divine blessings that has paved the way for the good things we receive from creation.

The note sounded in Deuteronomy 26 echoes throughout the Psalter as well. In its long list of divine blessings, Psalm 68 remembers:

> You showered rain in abundance, O God;
>   when your inheritance languished, you sustained it.
> Your creatures dwell there;
>   you sustain the needy through your goodness, O God.
> (vv. 9–10)

Psalm 65 strikes a similar chord when it declares:

> You visit the earth and water it;
>   you let it drink deeply;

> the channel of God is full of water.
> You provide their grain,
> > for thus you have ordained it.
> Watering its furrows,
> > leveling its ridges,
> you soften it with showers;
> > you bless its shoots.
> You crown the year with your goodness;
> > your wagon tracks drip with fatness.
> The oases of the wilderness drip with it;
> > and the hills are girded about with joy.
> The pastures are clothed with sheep,
> > and the valleys are covered with grain;
> > they shout and sing for joy!
>
> > > > (vv. 9–13)

But Israel and the promised land are not alone in enjoying God's blessings. All peoples share in his beneficence. Psalm 65:8 insists:

> Even those who dwell at the ends of the earth are in awe of your signs;
> > those where the morning and evening go forth shout for joy.

This is the idea picked up by Barnabas and Paul in Acts 14:17 when these missionaries to the Greeks insist that God "did not leave himself without a witness of doing good—giving you rain from heaven and fruitful seasons, satisfying your hearts with food and cheer." Jesus touches on this aspect of God's blessing as he says in the Sermon on the Mount:

> Love your enemies and pray for those who persecute you so that you can be children of your father who is in heaven; for he causes his sun to rise upon the evil and the good, and he sends rain upon the just and the unjust.
>
> > > > (Matt 5:44–45)

Biblical writers regard even the flora and fauna of the natural world as recipients of God's blessings. The majestic Psalm 104, which recasts in poetic form the prose creation account in Genesis 1, observes in verses 10–15:

> He sends forth springs in the wadis;
> > they make their way between the mountains.

> They give drink to all his creatures in the fields;
>> the wild donkeys quench their thirst.
> Beside them, the birds of the sky make their dwellings;
>> they send forth their voices from among the foliage.
> He waters the mountains from his upper chambers;
>> the earth is satisfied by the fruit of his works.
> He causes grass to sprout for the cattle,
>> and plants for humanity's labor,
> to bring forth bread from the earth,
>> and wine to rejoice the human heart,
> to make the face shine with oil,
>> and to strengthen the human heart with bread.

Verses 27–28 continue this theme:

> All of these wait for you,
>> to give them their food in its season.
> You give it to them, and they gather it up;
>> you open your hand, and they are satisfied with good things.

All of God's creation flourishes through God's continual blessing.

Conclusion

God's self-revelation in creation offers a vivid illustration of both his manifest presence and his elusiveness. On the one hand, a searching soul can find in creation undeniable evidence of God's presence and God's goodness. At the same time, a soul less disposed to search for God's presence can explain away a feature, however striking, as just the chance byproduct of an indifferent series of natural events. Perhaps this forms part of the reason why seeking is so vital to a proper understanding of God. God's presence is elusive; it must be sought to be found, even in creation.

5

Seeking God in Humanity

I praise you, for I am fearfully, wonderfully made;
　wonderful are your works;
　my soul knows it well!
My frame was not hidden from you
　when I was shaped in secret;
I was knit together in the recesses of the earth;
　Your eyes saw my unformed substance.
Upon your scroll were written, all of them,
　the days that were fashioned for me,
　and not one was missing.
　　　(Ps 139:14–16)

Not Good . . .

THE BIBLE'S CREATION STORIES ARE CANVASES on which the biblical authors sketch their most vivid images of the nature of God and of humanity. These are stories that tell us who God is, who we are, and what God expects of us. The depiction of God in these stories involves a complex interplay of God's transcendence and immanence. In Genesis 1, he is the God who merely speaks and sets creation flying to obey his will. With a word that is little more than a whisper in Hebrew (*yəhî*, a word that becomes the much clumsier "let there be" in English), God effortlessly masters the primordial chaos and sets creation in order. But God is also the deity of Genesis 2, a much more "earthy" God who plants a garden, makes the man out of dirt, breathes into his nostrils, fashions the woman from a rib, and walks with the first couple at day's end. It is the combination of these exalted and earthy elements in the divine nature that sets Judaism and Christianity apart from other religions' conceptions of God and gives them their unique theological stamp.

These same creation passages have much to say about the nature of humanity as well. Genesis 1 tells us that God made humanity male and female, that he made them in his image, and that he made them to continue his creative labors by exercising dominion over the earth (vv. 26–28). Genesis 2 touches on similar themes in its characteristically vivid narrative style. This second creation account doesn't mention the image of God explicitly, but it tells us that "the LORD God formed the man (*hā'ādām*) from the dust of the earth (*hā'ădāmâ*) and breathed into his nostrils the breath of life, and the man became a living being" (v. 7). Again, Genesis 2 doesn't record the particular divine command to exercise dominion over the earth, but it tells us the Lord God put the man in the garden of Eden "to work it and to keep it" (v. 15) and illustrates the man's authority over creation by giving him the task of naming the animals God had made (v. 19). This second chapter of Genesis also goes well beyond the first in its description of the interplay between the first man and the first woman in creation. Whereas Genesis 1 says merely that God made humans "male and female," in Genesis 2, the biblical writer famously narrates the woman's being formed from one of the man's ribs, the man's cry of delight at seeing her, and the divinely orchestrated union of the two as husband and wife.

Of particular interest is the author's explanation for *why* the woman was created. She was made, the author tells us, because the man by himself was inadequate. No sooner had God formed the man and placed him in the garden than he declared, "It is not good that the man should be alone" (v. 18). To remedy this problem, God then created a "helper corresponding to him." Unfortunately, both words in the Hebrew phrase *'ēzer kəneḡdô* are apt to be misunderstood. "Helper" (*'ēzer*) too readily connotes in English a subordinate or assistant, giving the misleading impression that the woman stands a step below the man. More often than not, though, the one who fills the role of *'ēzer* in the Bible is God himself. God is the *'ēzer* in Eben*ezer*, the "stone of help" that marks the Lord's help in battle. He is the father who *helps* Joseph (Gen 49:25), the one who *helps* Judah against his foes (Deut 33:7), the one who rides through the skies to *help* his people (v. 26). God is the *help* the psalmists constantly praise (Pss 10:14; 28:7; 33:20; 37:40; 54:4; 86:17; 115:9–11; 118:7, 13; 121:1–2; 124:8; 146:5), and the one whose *help* they earnestly seek (Pss 20:2; 30:10; 46:6; 70:5; 79:9; 109:26; 119:86, 173).[1] There is no more cause to imagine Eve as helper stood a step below Adam than to imagine God was diminished by his being a constant helper to his needy people.

The nature of the woman's "help" is clarified by the second term in the phrase. At the heart of *kənegdô* is the word *neged*, a term whose primary meaning is "opposite" or "in front of." In the context of Genesis 2, the sense of the term is one of the woman's standing opposite the man, in front of the man, face to face with him, and *corresponding* to him. The woman *matches* the man in a way that none of the animals paraded before him did (cf. vv. 19–20). It is this correspondence that is illustrated just a few verses later in the description of the couple's sexual union as becoming "one flesh" (v. 29). The man and the woman are not the same as one another, but their oppositions correspond in such a way that they complete each other. In a word, they "fit."

What is true of the man and the woman in the garden is true in a larger sense of humanity as a whole. When God looked at the isolation of the man, he declared that isolation to be "not good," and he took steps to remedy it by bringing the man into relationship with another person. Nature, even the paradisiacal form of nature in Eden, wasn't enough. God made human beings to live with one another.

Image-Bearers

It is interesting to consider why the creation account in Genesis 2 assesses the newly formed man and insists it wasn't good for him to be alone. There is the issue of procreation, of course, as the chapter culminates with the couple's becoming "one flesh." There is doubtless the matter of companionship, too. Certainly, there is more than just childbearing in the language of "bone of my bone and flesh of my flesh," "he shall cling to his wife," and "the two of them were naked, the man and his wife, but they were not ashamed" (vv. 23–25). If we add the account in Genesis 1 to the mix, then an additional possibility emerges as well. The very first poem in the Bible, Genesis 1:27, insists concerning humanity's creation:

> And God created the man in his image.
>   In the image of God he created him.
>   Male and female he created them.

God made us in *his* image; and if we are created in the image of God, then *we see something of God* when we see one another. There is a divine spark in humanity, placed there by God himself, and thus we see a reflection of the divine in the faces of our fellow human beings.

In the preceding chapter, we noted some of the various psalms that hold up *nature* as testament to God's great power and majesty. Psalm 8:1, for example, declares:

> O YHWH, our Lord,
>> how majestic is your name in all the earth,
>> for you have set your glory above the heavens.

But it's not just the natural world that displays God's glory; *humans* do so as well. Though, in one sense, humanity seems hardly worthy of notice when compared to the magnificence of God's creations in the heavens, the same psalmist insists:

> You have made them a little less than God,[2]
>> and you have crowned them with glory and honor.
> You have made them ruler over all the works of your hands;
>> you have put all things under their feet.
>>> (Ps 8:5–6)

Psalm 139:13–14 expresses these same sentiments:

> For you created my innermost being;
>> you knitted me together in my mother's womb.
> I praise you because I am fearfully, wonderfully made;[3]
>> wonderful are your works;
>> my soul knows very well.

As human beings, we are the pinnacle of God's creation. Honored by the psalmists with phrases like "a little less than God," "crowned with glory and honor," and "fearfully, wonderfully made," we stand alongside the stars and the mountains as God's handiwork and share in their created majesty.

Seeking God in Humanity

The companion to God's elusiveness—his rejection of all attempts to domesticate him or tie him down—is our need to seek after God. The Scriptures insist that seeking God is essential to gaining a proper understanding of who God is and to maintaining a right relationship with God. And though these same Scriptures serve as our primary avenue for seeking God, they also point to other ways of seeking him. God's creative works also point the way to him, and this includes the human beings God has created. As bearers of God's image, we reflect the divine countenance and offer one another an additional path for seeking God. But if this is the case, how can we search for God in our fellow human beings?

Look Past Humanity's Fallenness

We should stipulate from the outset that our search for God in the people he has made faces one enormous challenge. When we look at a natural wonder—a mountain or canyon, river or redwood—we don't have to raise a hand of reservation at its majesty. There is no "Yes, but . . . " when we marvel at the colors of a sunset. With humanity, this isn't the case. As God's children, we may bear his image, but we do so only imperfectly. Our fallenness has twisted and deformed that image so that we reflect the face of God in much the same way that a broken mirror reflects the face of the person standing before it.

At least in Oscar Wilde's classic novel, it was only Dorian Grey's *own* portrait that was marred by his crimes and vices. In the real world, our misdeeds often mar humanity's portrait of God himself. Accused by God of eating the forbidden fruit, Adam replied, "The woman *you gave* to be with me, she gave me of the tree and I ate" (Gen 3:12). We sin, but it is often God who is blamed—so much so that many people give up on God because they've given up on those who claim to be God's followers. There is, to be sure, a certain irony in a person's turning away from God because God's children are imperfect. The belief that human beings are sinful and in need of redemption is, after all, one of the central tenets of Christian theology. It seems odd that someone would give up on Christianity simply because one of its key claims has proved to be so manifestly true.

On the other hand, we do find in Scripture, especially in John's Gospel, the notion that God's revelation to humanity is mediated, first through his Son and secondarily through his Son's disciples. When Philip speaks for the disciples and asks Jesus to show them the Father, Jesus replies, "Have I been with you so long and yet you still do not know me, Philip? The one who has seen me has seen the Father!" (John 14:9). A few chapters later, in the so-called High Priestly Prayer, Jesus applies similar language to his disciples:

"As you have sent me into the world, so I have sent *them* into the world" (John 17:18). He goes on to say, "As you, Father, are in me and I in you, may *they* be in us, in order that the world may believe that you have sent me" (v. 21). He prays that the disciples may be one with one another "so that the world may know that you have sent me and have loved *them* just as you have loved *me*" (v. 23). Note especially Jesus' language in the phrases "that the world may believe" and "that the world may know." Jesus recognizes that the words and actions of the disciples will impact the way the world perceives him and, by extension, the way the world perceives the Father.

Finding God in our fellow human beings will require a bit of searching. We will have to burnish the tarnished surface of our humanity to find those things Paul described as true and honorable, just and pure (Phil 4:8). There is precedent in Scripture, though, for making just such an effort. We don't need to turn a blind eye to Paul's insistence that "all have sinned and fall short of the glory of God" to recognize moments when biblical authors look beyond human sinfulness to emphasize human *dignity* as well. The psalms noted above certainly do this, but so do many other passages. The same Paul who said "all have sinned" also refers to Gentiles who "by patience in doing good seek for glory and honor and immortality" and insists God will respond positively to those who do (Rom 2:6–7). Luke's description of Cornelius in the book of Acts surely falls into this category, as this Roman centurion is said to be "a devout man and one who fears God with all his household, doing many acts of charity for the people and praying constantly to God" (Acts 10:2). Alongside Cornelius, we might place Ruth, whose devotion and self-sacrifice fill every page of the book that bears her name, or Jethro, who proves to be not just father-in-law but trusted counselor to Moses.

In his Sermon on the Mount, Jesus also acknowledges that there can be goodness in humanity. When he encourages his followers to love their enemies, he holds up the example of the Father who "causes the sun to rise on the evil *and the good* and sends rain upon *the just* and the unjust" (Matt 5:45). Despite their failings, Jesus calls his disciples "friends" and sees good in people as varied as little children (Matt 19:14; Mark 10:14; Luke 18:16), a Canaanite woman in Syro-Phoenicia (Matt 15:28), a repentant tax collector (Luke 19:8–9), a tearful woman who anoints his feet (Luke 7:36–50), and a poor widow who gives her last two coins as an offering (Luke 21:1–4). He pushes his disciples to consider that even a Samaritan could show kindness to someone in need (Luke 10). Even as he is being crucified, Jesus looks at his tormentors and prays God's mercy upon them: "Father, forgive them, for they know not what they do" (Luke 23:34). To search for God in humanity will require us to have a similarly forgiving spirit—a spirit willing to recognize with Paul that we carry the treasure of the knowledge of God, but we do so in "jars of clay" (2 Cor 4:6).

Seek Out What Is Best *in Humanity*

Sadly, the fallenness of humanity is all too evident in our treatment of one another. Alongside our fallenness, though, there are also moments when even we mortals "get it right." Some of the most memorable parts of the stories we tell are those when a character's nobility shines through at just the right moment. (WARNING: The following pages contain multiple plot spoilers; read ahead at your own risk!) Few scenes in literature are more moving than the final pages of Dickens' *A Tale of Two Cities*.[4] As Charles Darnay spends his final hours in a prison cell, awaiting what will soon be his turn at the guillotine, Sydney Carton comes to visit. Carton is a rogue, a one-time rival for the affections of Darnay's wife, an acquaintance not a friend. And yet Carton tricks Darnay into changing places with him so that he may face execution and let Darnay return home to his family. As the tumbril carries Carton to his death, he is a changed man. He comforts a young seamstress about to meet the same fate. "Keep your eyes upon me, dear child," he says, "and mind no other object." When Carton's own moment arrives, he faces the blade with an expression of peace and even serenity. His thoughts look forward to a future in which Darnay and his wife, the woman Carton never ceased to love, are safely returned to England. He sees one of their future descendants bearing Carton's name in remembrance of his actions that day. He sees his name redeemed by this descendant: "I see the blots I threw upon it, faded away." And he says, in Dickens' famous closing words: "It is a far, far better thing that I do, than I have ever done; it is a far, far better rest that I go to than I have ever known."

Star Trek fans will recall the running theme of *A Tale of Two Cities* in the movie *The Wrath of Khan*. Early in the film, Spock gives a now (then?) antique copy of the book to Kirk on the occasion of his birthday. Kirk actually reads aloud the book's opening line: "It was the best of times, it was the worst of times." Though Spock denies his gift contains any hidden message, those in the audience know otherwise. Now an admiral, Kirk should be enjoying "the best of times," but trapped behind a desk rather than in the captain's seat where he belongs, the opposite is true. The spirit of the book emerges again in the climax of the movie as Spock sacrifices himself to save the ship. This leads Kirk in the movie's closing scene to quote the line mentioned above: "It is a far, far better thing that I do, than I have ever done; it is a far, far better rest that I go to than I have ever known."[5]

Tolkien's work is filled with these sorts of examples of self-sacrifice. We see it when Gandalf takes his stand on the bridge in Khazad-dûm, desperately fighting the Balrog to give his companions time to escape. We see it when Frodo and Sam press on toward Mount Doom even when it becomes clear that journeying forward will mean never journeying back. We see it with particular clarity in the case of Boromir. Only after he fails so spectacularly by trying to take the One Ring by force does he rediscover his true character and give his life in a valiant effort to save the Halflings. Tolkien describes the moment when Aragorn finds the great warrior:

> A mile, maybe, from Parth Galen in a little glade not far from the lake he found Boromir. He was sitting with his back to a great tree, as if he was resting. But Aragorn saw that he was pierced with many black-feathered arrows; his sword was still in his hand, but it was broken near the hilt; his horn cloven in two was at his side. Many Orcs lay slain, piled all about him and at his feet. Aragorn knelt beside him. Boromir opened his eyes and strove to speak. At last slow words came. "I tried to take the Ring from Frodo," he said. "I am sorry. I have paid."[6]

Stories like these register so powerfully with us because they echo *the* Story. Jesus once told his disciples, "No one has greater love than this, that one lay down one's life for one's friends" (John 15:13), and he went on to demonstrate this great love by laying down his own life for humanity. We hear echoes of what Jesus did for us when we hear of the sacrifices of Sydney Carton or Spock or Boromir or countless other examples besides.[7]

But it's not only in stories of dying for another that we see something of God. Jesus not only died for us; he also *lived* for us. His was a life of ministering to those in need. We find one particularly moving example of this in the first chapter of Mark's Gospel. The evangelist recounts the story of a leper who knelt before Jesus and said, "If you are willing, you can make me clean" (v. 40). The next verse captures the spirit of Jesus' ministry better than almost any other: "Moved with pity and stretching out his hand, he touched him and said to him, 'I am willing; be made clean!'" Every word of this verse is filled with theological significance: the tenderness of Jesus' heart as he is moved to pity by the man's suffering; the condescension (of a positive sort!) in his reaching out toward the man; his willingness to become ritually impure by touching a person stricken with leprosy; the comfort in the words "I am willing." This is the same sort of spirit we find in Philippians 2 as Paul describes the Messiah's ultimate act of condescension:

> Have the same mind among yourselves as was in Christ Jesus who, though he existed in the form of God, did not regard equality with God as something to be grasped, but emptied himself, taking the form of a slave, being born in the likeness of humans. And being found in the form of a man, he humbled himself and became obedient unto death, even death on a cross.
>
> (vv. 5–7)

When we see a person in a position of strength stoop down to offer kindness to a person in a position of weakness, we see something of the ministry of Jesus. We see something of the face of God.

In his well-known book *Mortal Lessons: Notes on the Art of Surgery*, Richard Selzer, a professor of surgery at Yale, recounts a particularly touching moment following a difficult facial operation. He had successfully removed a tumor from a young woman's cheek, but in the process an important nerve had been severed, leaving her mouth permanently contorted. Selzer describes the scene as the woman's husband stands beside her hospital bed:

> "Will my mouth always be like this?" she asks. "Yes," I say, "it will. It is because the nerve was cut." She nods and is silent. But the young man smiles. "I like it," he says, "It is kind of cute." All at once I *know* who he is. I understand, and I lower my gaze. One is not bold in an encounter with a god. Unmindful, he bends to kiss her crooked mouth and I so close I can see how he twists his own lips to accommodate to hers, to show her that their kiss still works. I remember that the gods appeared in ancient Greece as mortals, and I hold my breath and let the wonder in.[8]

Though we may not do so in prose as elegant as Selzer's, most of us can call to mind moments of similarly touching humanity. A hug given to a person fighting back tears of grief. A daughter gently brushing the hair of her elderly mother. A husband offering a hand of support to his aged wife. A good Samaritan stopping to help a stranger whose car has broken down. A teenager shielding a bullied student from further abuse. All of these are moments when charity toward others lets slip the mask of our humanity and reveals the face of God beneath.

Seek Out What Is **Beautiful** *in Humanity*

In the second act of *Hamlet*, the play's namesake confesses to Rosencrantz and Guildenstern that he has fallen into a sort of despondency that robs him of taking pleasure in even the most majestic elements of creation. Along the way, he offers an extraordinary ode to humanity itself:

> What a piece of work is a man! how noble in reason! how infinite in faculty! in form and moving how express and admirable! in action how like an angel! in apprehension how like a god! the beauty of the world! the paragon of animals! And yet, to me, what is this quintessence of dust? (*Hamlet*, act 2, scene 2)

Though his current melancholy might rob him of taking joy in humanity, Hamlet's (or should we say, the Bard's) own words make clear that there is much in humanity to be joyful about. The depths of our actions may be disturbingly deep, but we are capable of great heights as well. There is something noble, admirable, and even godlike in humanity. And in the same way that "the heavens declare the glory of God," so do we humans. What is beautiful in us is an echo of God's own beauty.

If we have eyes to see and ears to hear, we can catch a glimpse of something transcendent in the artistic accomplishments of our fellow brothers and sisters. To see the absolute mastery of the human form in Michelangelo's sculptures. The passion of his *Pietà*. The commanding gaze of his *David*. The stern resolve of his *Moses*. To marvel at the nearly photographic precision of Jan van Eyck's paintings. The impossible realism of the garments in his *Ghent Altarpiece*. The elegant details in his *Arnolfini Portrait* and his *Madonna in the Church*. To soar with the choral majesty of Beethoven's Ninth Symphony and its *Ode to Joy*. To feel the crushing weight of Mozart's *Requiem* and his *Don Giovanni*. To ache at the strains of Bach's aria "Erbarme dich, Mein Gott" ("Have Mercy, My God") in his *St. Matthew Passion*. We see God's reflection in these and countless other works.

Those who have seen the movie *The Shawshank Redemption* will recall a memorable scene in which a work of human beauty lifts even the hard men of Shawshank prison above the grind of their incarceration. To the utter consternation of the prison's guards and warden, the movie's lead character, Andy Dufresne, plays a glorious piece of classical music over the prison's loudspeakers: "*Canzonetta sull'aria*," a duet from Mozart's *Marriage of Figaro*. This information is lost on Andy's friend and the narrator of the movie, Morgan Freeman's character "Red." In Red's words:

> I have no idea to this day what those two Italian ladies were singing about. Truth is, I don't want to know. Some things are best left unsaid. I'd like to think they were singing about something so beautiful it can't be expressed in words and makes your heart ache because of it. I tell you those voices soared, higher and farther than anybody in a gray place dares to dream. It was like some beautiful bird flapped into our drab little cage and made those walls dissolve away, and for the briefest of moments, every last man at Shawshank felt free.

To see the scene in the movie, to watch each prisoner look upward, seemingly toward the loudspeaker but truthfully toward something beyond, is to see even in these grim men a glimpse of the divine.

Conclusion

No less than the rest of nature, God's human creations attest to both his presence and his elusiveness. Our own failings, manifestly evident in what Kant called "the crooked timber of humanity," often mar the image of God we each bear. A soul set to seek God in humanity will be forced to stumble over much that is fallen while we pursue something still upright. But that same soul set to seek after God can find evidence of God's greatness and his goodness in the people who surround us. If we look with forgiving hearts and love's willingness to bear, believe, and hope all things (1 Cor 13:7), we can see in our fellow brothers and sisters a still-lingering reflection of our Creator.

6

Seeking God in Worship

I rejoiced when they said to me,
    "Let us go to the house of the Lord*."*
        (Ps 122:1)

Better is one day in your courts
    than a thousand elsewhere.
I would choose rather to lie at the threshold of the house of my God
    than to live in the tents of the wicked.
        (Ps 84:10)

A Divided Nation

THE DEATH OF KING SOLOMON CREATED a crisis in the kingdom of Israel. Solomon was rightly famous for his wisdom, and his shrewd political skills led to a time of unprecedented prosperity in the land. A close reading of his story in 1 Kings, however, suggests the wise king's reign was not entirely positive. Solomon's many political marriages led him to build a host of shrines to deities other than Israel's true God, YHWH (1 Kgs 3:3; 11:1–8). And though he amassed wealth and power far greater than that of his father, David, that success came at a price. Solomon imposed forced labor on thousands of his own subjects to complete his many building projects (1 Kgs 5:13–14; 9:15–19). He exacted enormous taxes to supply the lavish demands of his royal table (1 Kgs 4:7, 22–23). On one occasion, he even gave away twenty northern Israelite cities to pay a debt to King Hiram of Tyre (1 Kgs 9:11). Solomon's growing despotism was sure to provoke a response, especially from the northern tribes who had suffered most under his rule. The moment news arrived that the old king had died, Jeroboam, one of Solomon's own former officials, launched a revolt, tearing ten of Israel's tribes away from the southern tribe of Judah.

Jeroboam's new dynasty wasn't meant to last. Though it had started with the support of various priests and prophets, Jeroboam soon ran afoul of both. To rival Solomon's temple in Jerusalem, Jeroboam built shrines of his own in Dan and Bethel, cities at the northern and southern edges of his kingdom. Israel had erected shrines before in towns like Shiloh, so building additional places of worship in the north wasn't unprecedented.[1] Jeroboam's choice of iconography for the shrines, however, could hardly have been worse. To rival Jerusalem's ark of the covenant, he adorned his two shrines with, of all things, golden calves. The response from the prophets and priests who had initially thrown their weight behind the revolt was immediate and harsh. Indeed, the story of the golden calf in Exodus 32 appears to have been written not just to condemn Aaron for his golden calf but to condemn Jeroboam for his calves as well.[2]

If Jeroboam's instincts were wrong when it came to the sorts of images he should place in his northern shrines, though, they were right in another respect. He understood with particular clarity how important worship would be for sustaining his kingdom. Three times a year, Israelite men were obliged to travel to Jerusalem, the city of David, to worship at the temple of Solomon. Jeroboam knew this state of affairs would put the survival of his own kingdom in serious jeopardy. We might suppose that Jeroboam's concerns were merely financial, as worshipers headed to Jerusalem would take their tithes and offerings there and create a drain on the northern kingdom. But this isn't how Jeroboam assessed the matter. Instead, he reasoned: "If this people keeps going up to make sacrifices at the house of the Lord in Jerusalem, *then the heart of this people might turn back to their lord there*, to Rehoboam the king of Judah" (1 Kgs 12:27). Jeroboam knew that *worship* centered in Jerusalem would foster *loyalty* to Jerusalem; only worship centered in the north could hope to create loyalty toward the north.

Habits of the Heart

I had the great blessing of doing my doctoral work in Boston. Boston is a wonderful city, steeped in history, full of great people, brimming with places to go and things to do. There is, of course, the weather, which is often abysmal, but the lovely fall months (nearly) make up for the lingering winter blues. One of the best parts of living in Boston is the sports scene. We were there when the Patriots began their multidecade reign over the NFL. Though, sadly, we left just before the Red Sox broke the "Curse" and won their first World Series in nearly a century, we got to see their rise from cellar dwellers to perennial contenders. It was a heady time to be a Boston sports fan. My sons and I seemed to know all the players, from Tom Brady to the reserve punter, from Big Papi to the latest middle reliever brought up from Triple-A.

Not surprisingly, moving away from Boston slowly chipped away at how wrapped up we were in the Pats and the Sox. Both teams still hold a special place in our hearts, but the rosters seem to shift and change so quickly that I can no longer keep track. My radio is no longer glued to the local sports station, so I don't get that daily dose of analysis on this leadoff batter's swing or that defensive end's pass rush. I can probably still list the starting roster from the Sox twenty years ago, but I would struggle to remember who took the field last year.

Most of us have those "remember when" moments that take us back to places that once were a regular part of our lives but now no longer are. We used to go to that vacation spot almost every year, but now it's hard to remember the last time we went. We used to be regulars at that restaurant, but it seems like ages since we last were there. It wasn't a bad experience that took us away. We didn't get bored with it exactly. One season of life just turned to another, and we drifted away. What once was a habit is now just a fond memory. What is true for a once-favorite vacation spot or a once-beloved restaurant can be true of our relationship with God as well. Something interrupts our habits and we begin to drift. If we drift too long, we drift away. If we drift too far, we have a hard time finding the way back.

Seeking God in Worship

Biblical authors recognized the importance of worship for holding fast to God. The psalmist who composed Psalm 42 expresses an intense sense of loss over the fact that he has, for reasons that remain unclear to us as readers, been deprived of the ability to join in worship with the rest of his people:

> These things I remember,
> > as I pour out my soul.
> > How I used to pass by with the throng,
> > > how I used to walk in procession with them to the house of God,[3]
> >
> > with a voice of joyous shouting and thanks,
> > > a multitude celebrating a festival.
>
> (v. 5)

It is this physical separation from the worshiping multitudes that evokes one of the most powerful lines in all of Scripture:

> As the deer pants for streams of water,
> > so my soul pants for you, O God!
>
> (v. 1)

Psalm 137 expresses similar sentiments when the songwriter laments:

> By the rivers of Babylon,
> > there we sat, there we wept,
> > when we remembered Zion.
>
> On the willows there
> > we hung our harps,
>
> for there our captors demanded of us
> > words of song,
>
> and our tormentors words of rejoicing:
> > "Sing for us one of the songs of Zion!"
>
> How could we sing the song of the Lord
> > in a foreign land?
>
> (vv. 1–4)

These are the words of worshipers heartbroken because of their separation from corporate worship of God.

Some of us experienced this pain of separation quite keenly during the lockdowns and social distancing associated with COVID. I leave it to others to opine on the wisdom of one public health response or another. My point is rather that whether by government mandate or personal caution, the pandemic threw up barriers to our gathering together for worship, and that loss of worshiping community continues to have profound impacts on both the church and society as a whole. It was Saint Augustine who famously said, "You have made us for yourself, O Lord, and our hearts are restless until they find rest in you" (*Confessions* 1.1). Worship is one of the means by which we can turn our restless hearts back toward God. But how can we actually seek God in worship?

Reaffirm Fundamental Truths

In our earlier discussion of seeking God in Scripture, we considered the particular word *meditate* (*hāgâ*) in Psalm 1:2. This is the term that has to do with deeply internalizing God's word so that it "bubbles up" from within us just when we need it. This is the same sentiment expressed in Psalm 119: "I have hidden your word in my heart, so that I might not sin against you" (v. 11). Our earliest spiritual ancestors saw the need to hear and recite, to read and memorize expressions of their most fundamental beliefs.

In a previous chapter, we considered the way Deuteronomy 26 encourages us to seek God in nature. There we saw that the ancient Israelites directly linked the bounty they received from the land to the blessing of God that made that bounty possible. This was the whole point, of course, of a "firstfruits" offering. But while Israel's various laws often prescribe these sorts of offerings, Deuteronomy 26 stands apart because of the declaration it insists must accompany the gift. Scholars have often noted that the words spoken here take the form of a creedal statement:[4]

> You shall declare before the Lord your God: "A wandering Aramean was my father. He went down to Egypt, and he sojourned there, few in number, but he became there a great nation, mighty and numerous. The Egyptians treated us harshly and oppressed us; and they imposed upon us hard labor. But we cried out to the Lord, the God of our fathers, and the Lord heard our cry and saw our misery and our trouble and our oppression. The Lord brought us out of Egypt with a mighty hand and an outstretched arm, with great terror and signs and wonders. He brought us to this place, and he gave us this land, a land flowing with milk and honey, and now I bring the first of the fruits of the ground that you gave me, O Lord!"
> (vv. 5–10)

Bringing the firstfruits to God was important, but not because the Israelites imagined that God himself needed the offering. As prophet and poet alike were eager to remind the people, God did not look to the Israelites for food (cf. Ps 50:8–13; Isa 1:11; Acts 17:24–25). Bringing firstfruits was important because *Israel* needed to remember who had given them this land and blessed it to be fruitful for the people. This was the point driven home by the declaration the people were to recite. The *words* that accompanied the message became the cord that tied act and belief together.

Various passages in the Hebrew Bible share the creedal quality of the declaration in Deuteronomy 26. In Deuteronomy 6:20–25, for example, part of the Mosaic sermon that introduces the book's law code, we find instructions for passing along the remembrance of God's deeds to the next generation. In times to come, when children ask about the laws the nation observes, the parental response should begin with the affirmation, "We were slaves to Pharaoh in Egypt, and the LORD brought us out of Egypt with a mighty hand" (v. 21). The enduring quality of this sort of language is evident in the fact that even to the present day these words form part of the liturgy recited at a Passover seder. The Hebrew words *ăḇāḏîm hāyînû ləp̄arʿô bəmiṣrāyim*, "We were slaves to Pharaoh in Egypt," punctuate the meal and set the stage for the corresponding reminder of God's deliverance.

These sorts of creedal statements quickly took root in the early Christian community as well. Most readers will already be familiar with statements of faith like the Apostles' Creed and the Nicene Creed. But similar sorts of fixed formulations of belief are also present already in the New Testament. In 2 Timothy 2:11–13, for example, Paul includes a statement about God's fidelity and our corresponding need to remain faithful to him:

> If we died with him, we will also live with him.
> If we endure, we will reign with him.
> If we deny, he will also deny us.
> If we are unfaithful, he remains faithful,
>   for he cannot deny himself.

The rhythmic cadence of these lines—a cadence even more evident in the underlying Greek text than in the English translation—already suggests a set liturgical piece. But any doubt on this point is removed when we consider that these lines are introduced with the words "faithful is the saying" (*pistos ho logos*). These words indicate that what follows is a statement of faith already in circulation in the early church. We find a similar example in Titus 3:4–8a as a tightly structured affirmation of God's mercy is accompanied by the same "faithful is the saying" formula, this time at the end rather than the beginning of the passage. Note also the carefully worded christological statement in 1 Timothy 3:16:

> He was revealed in flesh,
> vindicated in spirit,
> seen by angels,
> proclaimed among nations,
> believed on in the world,
> taken up into glory.

Though it lacks the "faithful is the saying" formula found in the preceding passages, the creedal character of the passage is nevertheless evident in the words that introduce the passage. Key is the term *homologoumenos*, which the New American Standard Version deftly translates as "by common confession." What follows is not just a matter of general agreement among believers, but a statement of shared theological belief.

We don't need to look far to find the motivation that stirred early believers to craft these sorts of creedal statements. These statements derive from a conviction that our most important truths need to be *repeated* again and again and again. This is the conviction that led Deuteronomy to command that the law be read every seven years at a celebration of the festival of Sukkoth (31:9–13). It's the conviction that eventually led Jews to insist that the Torah be read aloud in the synagogue, portion by portion, over the course of each year and to celebrate the completion of the readings with an annual festival called *Simchat Torah*—literally, "Rejoicing over Torah." Of course, to say that Simchat Torah celebrates the "completion" of the Torah readings is not strictly correct. The very moment that Deuteronomy 34, the last chapter of the Torah, is read, the scroll is rolled back to Genesis 1 so that the first chapter of the Torah can be read again. In a quite literal sense, the reading of Torah is never finished.

We know even from nonreligious settings that the repetition of fundamental truths can help in the formation of good habits and beliefs. One of the formative experiences of my youth was working to attain the rank of Eagle Scout. Indeed, I'm proud to say that I am the son of an Eagle Scout and the father of two Eagle Scouts. As I helped with my sons' Boy Scout troop, a fixture in our weekly meetings was the concluding ritual of gathering in a circle and reciting the Scout Oath, Law, and Motto. These last two were especially important for shaping the character of the young men in the troop. When the boys recited the Scout Motto—"Be prepared!"—they set out an expectation for how they should approach each outing we would take. As the boys said the Scout Law—"A Scout is trustworthy, loyal, helpful, friendly, courteous, kind, obedient, cheerful, thrifty, brave, clean, and reverent"—they were reciting a list of aspirational qualities we hoped to instill in each one of them. And when the occasion arose for one of these character qualities to be displayed, a leader or a fellow Scout needed only cite that quality from the Law to establish a shared sense of obligation. A boy who was tapped to say grace at a meal could simply say, "A Scout is reverent," and every Scout would remove his cap as a sign of respect. When it was time to gather firewood or clean up camp, the words "A Scout is helpful" were sufficient to get everyone involved. Our Scouts weren't perfect—what group of teenage boys is?—but there is no doubt that their character was shaped by their repetition of these key values.

What is true for these sorts of expressions in Scouting is equally true for more important truths. Reading and rereading the words of Scripture, repeating and repeating again the words of a catechism, memorizing and reciting the words of the ancient prayers and creeds—all of these actions tend to reprogram the software of our belief system. They work their way into our minds and, in time, even into our hearts. Some may object that these sorts of recitations run afoul of Jesus' admonition against what the King James Version labels "vain repetitions." This seems an odd objection given the fact that the very same Sermon on the Mount that contains this admonition (Matt 6:7) also contains the most frequently recited passage in all of Christianity, the Lord's Prayer (Matt 6:9–13). Jesus' command is not against repetition per se but against *meaningless* repetition, heaping up empty phrases. The words of Scripture and the key beliefs of our faith are neither meaningless nor empty. These are words that can reinforce our beliefs and provide safe houses for faith in times when the winds of struggle and doubt howl outside.

Sing!

Almost inextricably tied to the preceding idea is the notion that important truths are often best preserved in poetic and even musical form. This was certainly the case for the ancient Israelites. The great exodus miracle that God performed at the sea was preserved first in the *Song of the Sea* now found in Exodus 15; it was only later that the prose accounts of the sea crossing in chapter 14 were added. The same was true of Deborah's victory over Hazor in the book of Judges; the poetic Song of Deborah in Judges 5 was composed long before the later prose account found in chapter 4. Eventually, Israel's psalmists would set nearly the entirety of the nation's history to music in some of the Psalter's longest hymns; Psalms 78, 105, 106, 135, and 136 especially call on the people to remember and respond to God's great acts of deliverance over the centuries.

Just as they did with the creedal formulations noted above, early Christians followed the example of the Hebrew Scriptures in composing hymns. Many scholars believe Ephesians 5:14—"Awake, O sleeper, and rise from the dead, and Christ will shine on you!"—may be a fragment of an early baptismal hymn. Paul's memorable narration of Jesus' humiliation and subsequent exaltation in Philippians 2 is also widely regarded as an ancient christological hymn. Note the first part of this hymn as Paul urges the Philippians to act like Christ Jesus:

> Though he existed in the form of God,
> he thought not to cling to equality with God,
> but emptied himself,
> taking the form of a slave.
> And being born in the likeness of humanity,
> and found in appearance of man,
> he humbled himself,[5]
> being obedient even to death,
> even death on a cross.
>
> (vv. 6–8)

First Peter 2:22–25 is likely part of an ancient hymn as well, in this case, one modeled on the Suffering Servant hymns found in the book of Isaiah:

> Who committed no sin,
> neither was deceit found in his mouth.
> Who being reviled did not revile in turn.
> Suffering, he did not threaten,
> but rather entrusted himself to the one who judges justly.
> Who bore our sins in his body upon the tree,
> so that, free from sins, we might live for righteousness.
> By his wounds, you have been healed.
> For you, like sheep, were led astray,
> but now have been returned
> to the shepherd and guardian of your souls.

It's easy to see the value of these sorts of poetic renditions of beliefs and events. Poetry serves an artistic purpose, to be sure, but it is also invaluable as a mnemonic device. We remember what we can sing. This is the reason we often use songs to teach key ideas to children. The alphabet song has a permanent spot in most of our memories even though we've long since learned how to cycle through the alphabet without it. We still know the words to the song "Jesus Loves Me, This I Know," even though it may have been years since we last sang it. And learning from songs doesn't stop with childhood. I'm embarrassed to admit that I have a well-nigh encyclopedic knowledge of the lyrics of songs from the 1970s and '80s. I never set out to learn the words to these songs; truthfully, there are quite a few songs whose words I wish I could *unlearn*. But poetry, especially poetry set to music, has a way of getting in and refusing to get out.

Since we know this to be the case, it stands to reason that we can do ourselves a spiritual favor by opening the door for the *right* sort of music and poetry into our hearts. By "right," I certainly make no claims about whether one style of music is superior to another. Almost any style of music we listen to today will be dramatically different than the forms our audiences in the Bible would have known. My concern is rather with two particular values: content and connection. In terms of content, if we know that the words we sing will shape our minds, then we certainly want to make sure those words reinforce true ideas rather than false ones. In terms of connection, though a great many psalms urge us to sing a "new song" to the Lord (Pss 33:3; 96:1; 98:1; 144:9; 149:1), there is surely some benefit as well to singing songs that connect us with the great river of tradition that has been passed down over the centuries. Singing new songs need not force us to sever our worshiping connection with the long line of believers who came before us.

Embrace the Power of Ritual

One passage we could easily add to the creedal statements discussed above is Deuteronomy 6:4–5: "Hear, O Israel, the Lord is our God, the Lord is one. And you shall love the Lord your God with all your heart, with all your soul, and with all your strength." This famous text is known as the *Shema*, a name derived from the Hebrew imperative "Hear!" that introduces the first part of this declaration: *šəmaʿ yiśrāʾēl YHWH ʾĕlōhênû YHWH ʾeḥād*. These are the words Jesus sets forth as the greatest commandment when pressed by one of the scribes (Mark 12:29). They are the words that observant Jews continue to pray every morning and evening. They are the words that hung on the dying lips of a martyr like Rabbi Akiva after the Bar Kochbah revolt and that form the final prayer of a man about to die even in a modern fictional setting like the Israeli television series *Fauda*.[6]

As important as these words are, we should take note of the fact that Deuteronomy is not content merely to assert that the Lord is one or to command that Israel love him. The book goes on to insist on particular *ways* in which the people are to remind themselves of this conviction and this duty. In verses 6–8 of the same passage, Moses is said to urge the people:

> These words that I am commanding you today shall be upon your heart. You shall repeat them to your sons and speak them when you stay at home and when you go out upon the way, when you lie down and when you rise up. You shall inscribe them as a sign upon your hand and a symbol between your eyes. You shall write them upon the doorposts of your house and upon your gates.
>
> (Deut 6:6–8)

In these verses, belief (that God is one) and attitude (love for God) are wedded to *action*. In some Jewish traditions, these actions are performed quite literally, as the faithful recite the words of the Shema before going to bed ("when you lie down") and again during morning prayers ("when you rise up"). Pieces of parchment containing verses from Deuteronomy and other texts are placed in small holders called *mezuzot* (literally, "doorposts") and affixed to doorways. Other pieces are placed in small leather boxes called *tefillin* and worn on the arms and forehead during prayer.

Although not every tradition even within Judaism follows each of these practices, there is nonetheless something instructive in them. They illustrate the quite biblical notion that *doing* fosters *believing*. Just in Deuteronomy, we find instructions to keep the Sabbath (5:12–15), to remove images of other gods (12:2–3), to obey particular food laws (14:3–21), to set aside tithes from the field and firstlings from the flock (14:22–29), to make pilgrimages to the temple for special festivals (16:16–17), and to bring offerings of firstfruits to God (26:1–10). In other words, Deuteronomy creates a world of *ritual* to reinforce belief.

My own spiritual roots trace back to what one might call "low-church Protestantism." We had Communion not the Eucharist, grape juice not wine, altar calls not altar boys, brothers not bishops. Pipe organs and pastoral robes were a bit too highbrow for the likes of us, and we certainly didn't follow the lectionary or the liturgical calendar (unless Christmas and Easter alone can be called a "liturgical calendar"). Some in my church probably would have claimed that we eschewed ritual altogether, but this, of course, wasn't true in the slightest. An ecclesiastical scholar examining our bulletins from week to week would have found a regularity nearly as unchangeable as the Latin Rite. We just hesitated to *admit* that our repeated practices were rituals. To our minds, rituals tended to deaden faith, and that was why we believed the New Testament had deliberately made a break with that sort of religion in favor of the relationship at the heart of Christianity.

There is, to be sure, a worthy caution in low-church Protestantism's concerns about ritual. Ritual is quite capable of serving as a substitute for authentic spiritual commitment. This was a persistent complaint among Israel's prophets as they found sacrifices and worship divorced from faith and faithfulness to be not just ineffectual but actually *provocative* to God. The prophet Isaiah, for example, conveys the divine accusation:

> This people draws near to me with their mouths,
>   and honors me with their lips,
>   but their hearts are far from me.
> And their fear of me
>   is but a human commandment they have been taught.
>
>   (29:13)

Centuries later, Jesus turned the prophet's words against his own opponents when he found a particular practice legal but hypocritical (cf. Matt 15:7–9).

These valid cautions aside, though, there is more to the ritual story than I and my fellow church members might have been willing to admit. From the outset, it bears noting that ritual is not confined to the Old Testament, nor is it merely the invention of some medieval pope or patriarch; the New Testament itself contains (and commands!) a great deal of ritual. Regular corporate worship (Heb 10:25; Acts 2:42), the celebration of the Lord's Supper (1 Cor 10:21; 11:20–34), the public reading of Scripture (1 Tim 4:13), preaching and teaching (1 Cor 11:1–16; 1 Tim 4:13; 2 Tim 4:2; Titus 2:15), prayer (Eph 6:18; Phil 4:6; Col 4:2; 1 Tim 2:1–8; Jas 5:13–18), anointing the sick (Jas 5:14), baptism (Matt 28:19; Acts 22:16; Rom 6:3–4; 1 Cor 12:13; Gal 3:27; Eph 4:5; Col 2:12), singing (1 Cor 14:26; Eph 5:19; Col 3:16; Jas 5:13), greeting with a holy kiss (Rom 16:16; 1 Cor 16:20; 2 Cor 13:12; 1 Thess 5:26; 1 Pet 5:14)—all of these are ritual practices, and all are found in the New Testament (and we could easily add to this list practices like marriage and offices like bishop, elder, deacon, and so forth, all of which are found in the New Testament).

One could argue whether these New Testament practices are intended to be exhaustive (no new practices should be added) or merely representative (new rituals could develop in different places and different times). What can't be argued, though, is that the authors of the New Testament abandoned ritual altogether; they clearly did not. Those who wish to walk in the footsteps of our spiritual ancestors, Old Testament and New, would do well to consider how action can certify belief and how ritual can solidify faith.

Conclusion

If New Testament authors did raise concerns about ritual, their concerns were essentially the same as those set forth by the Hebrew prophets—namely, that ritual *acts* ought to be accompanied by devoted *hearts*. This, of course, is the heart of Jesus' reinterpretation of the law in his Sermon on the Mount. As Jesus expanded the command concerning murder to include anger (Matt 5:21–26) and the command concerning adultery to include lust (5:27–30), he was insisting on a marriage of body *and* heart in obedience to God. This is the same issue that is at stake in his encounter with the so-called rich young ruler. Jesus didn't object in the slightest to the young man's claim that he had diligently kept the law's requirements; instead, he zeroed in on the weak spot in the man's devotion to God, challenging him to go beyond mere obedience to full commitment (cf. Matt 19:16–22).

There is a flip side to this emphasis on the union of action and belief in ritual and, by extension, to our earlier discussion of repeating and reaffirming important truths. There are times when belief wavers and what we need is a lifeline that can keep us steady in a difficult moment. Students of the Gospels will surely remember the occasion when Jesus walked out on the waters of the Sea of Galilee to meet the struggling disciples (Matt 14:25–33). Ever the boldest disciple, Peter saw Jesus on the water and asked permission to join him. Jesus told him to come, and for a moment Peter, too, was able to walk on the sea. But feeling the daunting wind and seeing the buffeting waves, Peter wavered and began to sink. Jesus' disappointment with Peter was clear as he said, "You of little faith, why did you doubt?" Despite Peter's flagging faith, though, Jesus also reached out, took him by the hand, and caught him. What Jesus did for Peter in that moment, ritual and creedal reaffirmation have the potential to do for us as well. In those moments when God's elusiveness seems too much to bear, in those moments when the groaning of creation is our groaning, too, a pattern of faithful actions, repeated even when we don't "feel like it," can keep us moving in the right direction.

7

Seeking God in Silence

Be silent, all flesh, before the LORD,
  for he stirs from his holy dwelling!
    (Zech 2:13)

The LORD *is in his holy temple;*
  be silent before him, all the earth!
    (Hab 2:20)

A Dangerous Prosperity

WITH THE BENEFIT OF HINDSIGHT, WE might well call the opening decades of the eighth century BC the calm before the storm. Soon, the mighty empires of Mesopotamia would stir from long periods of decline, and Israel would come to suffer centuries of domination at the hands of the Assyrians, Babylonians, and Persians. For a moment, though, the nation enjoyed a time of relative peace.

This peace was matched by almost unprecedented prosperity. In popular imagination, the land of Israel is often cast as an austere place of forbidding rocks and waterless desert. While there is land to match this description in the south of the country, the northern part of Israel is a different place entirely. Here, the landscape resembles nothing so much as

California's Napa Valley. Rain is plentiful in this region—the Upper Galilee actually receives more rain each year than London or Seattle—and waters from gushing springs like those at Dan and Banias go on to nourish the land's rolling fields and farmlands.[1]

Unfortunately, the north's prosperity during this period did not produce a return to Eden. The prophet Amos traveled up from the southern kingdom of Judah to offer a withering critique of Israel's oppression of the poor and exploitation of the vulnerable. Prosperity wouldn't last, he insisted, if it wasn't coupled with justice (cf. Amos 2:6–8; 5:10–12, 21–24). The prophet Hosea also railed against the north, though his criticisms were more theological than ethical. When Hosea pointed an accusing finger against Israel, it was to charge the people with attributing their great prosperity to the wrong god:

> For she [Israel] said, "I will go after my lovers,
>   the ones who give me my bread and my water,
>   my wool and my flax, my oil and my drink." . . .
> But she did not know
>   that it was I who gave to her
>   the grain and the new wine and the oil.
> The silver and the gold I multiplied for her,
>   they used for Baal.
>
> (Hos 2:5, 8)

It was YHWH, the God of Israel, who gave the people their grain, wine, and oil, but the recipients of the Lord's blessing attributed their abundance instead to Baal.

On one level, Baal's attraction for the people of Israel is not that hard to understand. As the supposed god of the thunderstorm, it was easy to imagine that Baal was the deity who sent the life-giving rains for the farmers' fields. His cult proved incredibly popular in the coastal regions of Lebanon and Syria, Israel's neighbors to the north, so it's no surprise that he developed a following in Israel as well. Israel's true God, though, would have none of it. Picking up on an image used in various places in Scripture, Hosea casts the relationship between God and Israel as one of husband and wife. When Israel lavishes her affections on Baal, God promises to respond as an aggrieved husband and strip away the favors he had given her:

> "I will put an end to all her rejoicing,
>   her festivals, her new moons, and her sabbaths,

and all her appointed assemblies.
I will lay waste to her vines and her fig trees,
    of which she said, 'These were a gift to me,
    my lovers gave them to me.'
I will turn them into a forest,
    and beasts of the field will eat them.
I will visit upon her all the days of the Baals,
    when she would offer incense to them.
She adorned herself with rings and ornaments,
    and went after her lovers,
    but me she forgot," declares the LORD.
                    (Hos 2:11–13)

At one point, God seemingly goes so far as to divorce Israel: "You are not my people," he says, "and I am not your God" (Hos 1:9).

The relationship between God and Israel appeared to rest on a knife's edge. But in keeping with the strong marital imagery employed in the book, God announces his intention to woo the nation all over again:

Therefore, behold, I will allure her,
    and draw her back to the wilderness,
    and speak to her heart. . . .
She will respond there as she did in the days of her youth,
    as she did when she came up from the land of Egypt.
                    (Hos 2:14–15)

Of particular note is the *place* where God intends to court the nation once more. Like a struggling married couple who return to the place of their honeymoon to rekindle their romance, God says he will take Israel back to the desert where their relationship was first consummated. Prosperity had proved too much for the nation. For the people to find God again, they needed to return to a place marked by want rather than abundance, by isolation rather than crowds, by silence rather than busy streets and marketplaces. *They needed to return to the wilderness.*

Time in the Wilderness

I confess that I have a soft spot for the desert. My wife loves the Galilee, and I certainly can't deny the charms of its lovely hills and farms. Somehow, though, my heart always returns to the desert. The stark beauty of the chalk and limestone cliffs of Wadi Ein Avdat. The dramatic overlooks of the Makhtesh at Mitzpe Ramon. The somber quiet of Masada. The burst of vegetation that jostles for a spot around the waters at Ein Gedi. These are the locales that seem to draw me back again and again. Standing alone, looking across the subtle contours of the desert hills and valleys, I am finally able to immerse myself in a kind of silence few other places provide. The cares that dominate ordinary life slip away, and my mind is at last able to find a moment's rest.

This is not to say the wilderness is an easy place. Quite the contrary. The wilderness doesn't suffer fools. It shows little mercy to those who venture in unprepared for its privations. We see this in Scripture on several occasions as those unaccustomed to life in the wilderness are suddenly forced to reckon with its challenges. In Genesis 21, when Sarah perceived Ishmael and his "laughter" (Hebrew *məṣaḥēq*) to be a threat to her own "laughter," Isaac (Hebrew *yiṣḥāq*), she insisted that Abraham send Ishmael and his mother, Hagar, away. Reluctantly, Abraham agreed to do so. He supplied Hagar and Ishmael with food and a skin of water and watched as they made their way into the wilderness. In the span of only a single verse in the chapter (v. 15), mother and son find themselves in desperate straits. Their water gone, Hagar sets Ishmael under a bush and retires to a spot a short distance away so she can be spared from having to watch the boy die. Ultimately, it takes an angelic intervention to rescue the pair and open Hagar's eyes to see the well of water that had apparently been there all along (cf. v. 19).

At first glance, it might strike us as quite odd that Hagar was so quickly at a loss in the wilderness. Accustomed, as we often are, to imagining that nearly all of ancient Israel was desert and nearly all its inhabitants desert dwellers, we might find it hard to understand how Hagar could prove so ill-suited to life in the wilderness. The fact is, though, that biblical Israel was not entirely or even mostly desert, nor were its people mainly the ancient equivalent of Bedouin tribes. It's true that Abraham and his family seem to have lived a semi-nomadic lifestyle, with seasonal or at least periodic movements from one locale to another, but these early Hebrew patriarchs were the exception, not the rule. More important even than this, though, is the fact that Hagar wasn't a Hebrew at all; she was an Egyptian. However prepared for wilderness life Abraham may have been, his Egyptian concubine would not have shared his desert skills. Egypt is the Nile, and life near the Nile is the very opposite of desert life.

The remarkable ruins at Sepphoris in the lower Galilee preserve a mosaic depicting what is called a "Nilometer," a marker that both measured the height of the Nile's flow and specified the corresponding rate of the nation's taxes. So predictable was the nation's agriculture that administrators knew a full Nile meant steady irrigation and thus bountiful crops to tax. As an Egyptian, Hagar would have been accustomed to the regularity of the Nile's flow and the dependability of its water supply. In the wilderness, this predictability was gone, and Hagar and Ishmael were soon in desperate need of rescue.

What was true for Hagar was equally true for the Israelites who experienced the exodus. Though the early chapters of the book of Exodus repeatedly emphasize the harshness of the Egyptians' oppression of their Israelite slaves (cf. Exod 1:13–14; 2:23; 3:7), there was a predictability to life in Egypt that the nation would come to miss during their desert sojourn. Just one chapter after the nation's miraculous crossing of the sea, they cry out over their lack of food:

> Would that we had died by the hand of the LORD in the land of Egypt, where we sat beside pots of meat and ate bread to our fill! For you have brought us out to this wilderness to kill this whole congregation with hunger!
>
> (Exod 16:3)

Later they voice similar complaints about the food:

> We remember the fish that we ate in Egypt for free! The cucumbers, the melons, the leeks, the onions, and the garlic!
>
> (Num 11:5)

And the people's complaints about water in the wilderness are perhaps even more intense:

> Why did you bring us up from Egypt to take us to this evil place? There is no place for seed or fig or vine or pomegranate, and there is no water to drink!
>
> (Num 20:5)

> The people spoke against God and against Moses, saying, "Why did you bring us up from Egypt to kill us in the wilderness? For there is no bread and no water, and our throats are disgusted with this miserable bread!"
>
> (Num 21:5)

> The people thirsted there for water, and they complained against Moses. They said, "Why did you bring us up out of Egypt to kill us and our children and our cattle with thirst!"
>
> (Exod 17:3)

Though the role of the wilderness in Scripture can hardly be overstated, the Israelites themselves showed little affection for it. Theirs were the sentiments expressed by Prince Faisal (Alec Guinness) to T. E. Lawrence (Peter O'Toole) in the movie *Lawrence of Arabia*:

> I think you are another of these desert-loving English. Gordon of Khartoum. No Arab loves the desert. We love water and green trees. There's nothing in the desert. No man needs nothing.

It would be wrong to say that the ancient Israelites loved the desert. Their time in the wilderness was a matter of necessity, not preference. In part, this necessity was political. When neighboring countries proved more powerful than Israel, they grabbed the fertile north and the coastal plain for themselves, forcing the Israelites to seek shelter in the central mountains and southern deserts. This necessity was also spiritual, though. Prosperity didn't always agree with Israel's spiritual health. The challenges of the wilderness often proved more suitable for finding God and learning to trust in him.

From Eden to Abraham

The pervasiveness of the wilderness motif in Scripture is so great that we are apt to miss it in the same way we might miss the proverbial forest for the trees. Consider that the first couple of creation is set in a garden, the very Garden of Eden, surrounded by "every tree that is pleasant to look upon and good for food" (Gen 2:9), yet they turn almost immediately away from God's command and toward their own desires. Their descendants fare a little better as they replace the garden's abundance with cities and civilizations of their own design. From murderous Cain who builds the first city (Gen 4:17) to the rebellious city-builders at Babel (Gen 11:4), humanity in the protological narratives of Genesis 1–11 grows increasingly hostile to God and God's vision for human flourishing.

And then God calls Abraham. From the fertile seedbed of empires in Mesopotamia, God sends Abraham (still Abram at this point) to the land that would become Israel (Gen 12:1). But God doesn't lead Abraham to just to any part of Israel; he guides him to the stretch of land that runs from the rugged hills near Bethel down to the arid region of Beersheva. God takes Abraham to the wilderness. It is there in the wilderness that Abraham learns to trust God and there that God marks a new turn in his relationship with humanity.

Moses

Abraham's descendants go on to have their own wilderness experiences. Save for the Messiah himself, no figure looms larger over the biblical narrative than the great lawgiver Moses. Moses is the one of whom God said, "I know you by name" (Exod 33:12). He's the one the Lord knew "face to face" (Deut 34:10). And yet, Moses is also one of the Bible's great tragic figures.[2] Though he may have been rescued by Pharaoh's daughter and raised in Pharaoh's household, Moses was no "prince of Egypt." When Pharaoh learned that Moses had killed an Egyptian, he actually sought to kill Moses, something he would never have done had Moses been the "second son" portrayed on stage and screen. But if Moses didn't belong to Egypt, it is equally clear that he didn't truly belong to Israel. Moses may have been moved by his people's labors, but he didn't actually share them. When he tried to break up the fight between one Hebrew and another, the man who was in the wrong demanded of Moses, "Who made you a prince and a judge over us?" The man may have been in the wrong as it concerned his fellow Hebrew, but he was largely right concerning Moses: *No one* had made Moses a prince or judge over the Israelites. Moses was an outsider to his own people. He was a man without a country.

Truthfully, there was only one place where Moses found a home for himself—in the wilderness of Midian. It was in Midian that Moses rescued Jethro's daughters from the harassment of a band of shepherds, and it was in Midian that he married one of those daughters, Zipporah, and welcomed a son into his family. Significantly, Moses gave his son the name Gershom. Whatever the technical etymology of Gershom may be, it is clear that Moses himself had a particular folk meaning in mind for the name. He named his son Gershom, saying, "I have been a stranger (Hebrew *gēr*) in a foreign land." Moses looked back to Egypt and rightly recognized that he hadn't belonged "there" (*shom* in the name Gershom is a wordplay on the Hebrew *šām*, "there"). He had been a stranger among both Egyptians and Hebrews. It was in the desert that Moses found his home, and it was in the desert that

Moses eventually found God. Alone in the wilderness, tending his father-in-law's sheep, Moses was met by God at the famous burning bush. It would not be long before he would bring the entire nation back to this spot for their own wilderness encounter with God.

The Exodus Generation

The wilderness wanderings of the Israelites after their exodus from Egypt are surely the most famous desert experience in all of Scripture, and with good reason. Not only is Israel's time in the desert the longest of these experiences—a full forty years—but it is there in the wilderness that we see most vividly the terms under which God would remain in relationship with his people. It is in the wilderness that God lays out most forcefully his insistence that Israel would be his people and he their God *if and only if* they were willing to place their unconditional trust in him. When the people lack food and water in the wilderness, they must trust God to provide for them. When they are attacked by mightier and more vicious foes, they must trust God to protect them. When they are confused and afraid, they must trust God to lead them. Sadly, the generation that experienced the great acts of deliverance in the exodus never came to trust in God. And as God would remain in relationship with the people on no other terms, that generation was left to live out their remaining years in the desert. It would be left to their children to finally commit themselves to God's promises and take the land their parents had refused.

Elijah

Nearly everyone has heard of Elijah's famous contest with the prophets of Baal. The fire that rains down from heaven and consumes the sacrifice at Carmel is one of the Bible's most memorable stories. Less familiar, perhaps, is the story that follows in the wake of this great contest. When the infamous Queen Jezebel hears of Elijah's victory and the death of her Baal prophets, she issues a threat against the Lord's own prophet: "Thus may the gods do to me and more also if by this time tomorrow I do not make your life like one of theirs!" (1 Kgs 19:2). Fearing for his life, Elijah is forced to retreat to the wilderness around Beersheva. There, the prophet has to wrestle with his own issues of trust. Echoing the Israelites who cried out, "Would that we had died in Egypt!" when they were short on food and water, Elijah laments, "Enough! Now, O Lord, take my life, for I am no better than my ancestors!"

(v. 4). And just as God provided the Israelites with manna from heaven and water from a rock, an angel provides Elijah with a loaf of bread baked on a rock and a jar of water. But Elijah finds more than just miraculous food and drink in the wilderness. It is there that he has an encounter with God himself. The ministering angel says to the prophet, "Go out and stand on the mountain before the LORD, for the LORD is about to pass by" (v. 11a). Note the manner in which God appears:

> A great and mighty wind was tearing apart mountains and shattering rocks before the LORD. But the LORD was not in the wind. And after the wind, an earthquake. But the LORD was not in the earthquake. And after the earthquake, fire. But the LORD was not in the fire. And after the fire, a sound of sheer silence.
>
> (vv. 11b–12)

When Moses encountered God, the Lord said, "You shall see my back, but my face shall not be seen" (Exod 33:23). With Elijah, God's appearance is even more mysterious; he appears but only in the "sheer silence" that Elijah experiences. Like Moses, Elijah both sees and does not see; though he encounters God, God remains elusive. But even this elusive theophany is important as it prepares Elijah to take on Ahab and bring his idolatrous dynasty to an end.

Others Still

Once we start looking, it is striking to see just how often wilderness experiences figure in the lives of key biblical characters. We might think of Jacob, for example, when he stole his brother's blessing and was forced to flee to Mesopotamia. It was while he was alone on the journey away from Beersheva that Jacob first experienced God's presence (Gen 28:11–22). On his return journey, still alone in the wilderness, he experienced God's presence again, this time as he wrestled with God (Gen 32:24–32). Alongside Jacob we could place mighty King David. Before David was king, he was first a servant to King Saul. When Saul became convinced that David posed a threat to his family, David was forced to flee to the wilderness around Ein Gedi. In his later years, he reflected on his wilderness escape from Saul:

> In my distress, I called to the LORD,
>   and to my God I called.
> He heard my voice in his temple,

>   my cry was in his ears. . . .
> He reached down from on high, he took me;
>   he drew me up from mighty waters.
> He rescued me from my strong enemy,
>   from those who hate me,
>   for they were too strong for me.
>
>   (2 Sam 22:7, 17–18)

Lastly, we should note that the New Testament is not without its own desert experiences. The apostle Paul recounts that after his encounter with the risen Jesus, he "went away into Arabia," a time he claimed was even more formative for his ministry than his eventual consultations with Peter and the other disciples in Jerusalem (Gal 1:17). And, of course, there is the most famous wilderness experience in the New Testament, that of Jesus himself.

Seeking God in Silence

In each of the Synoptic Gospels—Matthew, Mark, and Luke—Jesus' ministry formally begins when he is baptized by John at the Jordan River. Importantly, each of these Gospels notes that Jesus' baptism wasn't immediately followed by teaching the masses or healing the sick. Instead, Jesus was first driven by the Spirit into the wilderness. Even the Messiah needed the refining experience of the wilderness to prepare him for the challenges that lay ahead. There are lessons for us as well in his desert sojourn.

Searching Alone

In the preceding chapter, we discussed the fact that worship is one of the means by which we can search for God. There is value, inestimable value in walking alongside others who are also on a pilgrim's trail of seeking God's face. But however valuable the company of fellow travelers may be, much of our search for God will have to be done alone. If we intend to seek God—God himself and not merely church, God himself and not merely community, God himself and not merely the experience of worship—if we intend to seek *God*, then we will have to seek him by ourselves.

A close reading of the Gospels' temptation narratives shows that this was the case for Jesus as well. In each one of the Synoptics, Jesus' journey into the wilderness takes place at the Spirit's prompting, though, truthfully, "prompting" may be too gentle a term for the Spirit's leading. Mark tells us that "the Spirit *drove* Jesus into the wilderness" (1:12). It does not appear, however, that the Spirit who drove Jesus into the desert remained with him once he was there. It was only after the forty days of hunger and thirst, after the difficult temptations proffered by Satan, that Jesus again received divine comfort. As both Matthew and Mark indicate, it was only at the end of Jesus' time of trial that angels came to attend to him (cf. Matt 4:11; Mark 1:13). Jesus had to go through his testing alone.

In a movie full of memorable songs, the Fairfield Four's rendition of "Lonesome Valley" in *O Brother, Where Art Thou?* is particularly striking. Though the song is nearly a century old and has been covered by all manner of country, gospel, and folk singers, the wedding of the quartet's deep bass harmonies and melancholy gravedigging gives the song a powerful, haunting quality:

> You got to go to the lonesome valley.
> You got to go there by yourself.
> Nobody else can go for you.
> You got to go there by yourself.
> Oh, you got to ask the Lord's forgiveness.
> Nobody else can ask him for you.
> You got to go to the lonesome valley.
> You got to go there by yourself.
> Nobody else, nobody else can go for you.
> You got to go there by yourself.

Though the "lonesome valley" in this memorable song describes the death each person must face alone and the accounting each soul must give, its language applies with equal force to the search for God. No one else can go for you. Those who seek God's face have to walk through the lonesome valley by themselves.

Never Been More Difficult

The fact that much of our seeking after God must be done alone poses a particular challenge in this day and age. There has never been a time when it has been more difficult to be *truly* alone.

I've been privileged to travel to a great many places that once were decidedly remote. I've walked among the towering trees of Muir Woods and

Redwood National Park, stared in amazement at the crystal blue waters of Crater Lake, marveled at Olympic's waterfalls and Hall of Mosses, and driven untold hundreds of miles in Yellowstone. In not one of these places, though, have I ever been alone. Other travelers, just as eager to see the sites, invariably crowd along the same roads and trails that brought me there. At Yosemite, the National Park Service at least makes an attempt to create space for solitude by requiring wilderness permits to visit certain areas. Only a handful of people are allowed in at the various trailheads. Yet even with this careful distribution of visitors, you still see a half-dozen groups each day along the trail. And beyond those direct encounters with other people, there is also the fact that even in the backcountry of this great wilderness preserve, trucks can be heard on distant highways, airplanes fly overhead, and cellphone service is increasingly ready to hand.

To be alone today will demand a concerted effort. It will require setting aside phone, tablet, laptop, television, and radio. It will require a deliberate and methodical *untethering* from the world around us. And the world around us will not go gentle into that good night. There will always be a text, a notification, a call, a digital reminder, a new episode competing for our attention. Jesus' own time in the wilderness seems to have been a last gasp of solitude before the pressures of his ministry would make being alone nearly impossible for him. As he began to teach and to preach, to heal and to serve, Jesus was hounded by seemingly insatiable crowds. Mark tells us that on one occasion, "He told his disciples to have a boat ready for him on account of the crowd, so that they would not crush him" (Mark 3:9). Matthew recalls another occasion when Jesus attempted to withdraw in a boat "to a deserted place by himself" but could not because "when the crowds heard it, they followed him on foot from the towns" (Matt 14:13).

And when it wasn't the crowds that forced themselves on Jesus, it was Jesus' own compassion for the crowds that compelled him to give up his retreat. Again, Matthew tells us, "When he went forth, he saw a great crowd, and he had compassion for them and healed their sick" (Matt 14:14). Eventually, Jesus ended up feeding the multitudes—five thousand men, besides women and children—and sending the disciples on their way while he dismissed the people. At last, he was alone. Matthew tells us Jesus "went up the mountain by himself to pray" (v. 23). But Jesus had hardly found his mountainside spot when he saw his disciples struggling in the boat against an adverse wind. Once more, Jesus' compassion got the better of him, and he went to the disciples, famously walking on the water to meet them (vv. 22–25).

Though it was difficult for Jesus to find moments of solace and retreat, that didn't stop him from trying to seek them out. Luke tells us:

> The word about Jesus spread more than ever, and great crowds gathered about him to hear him and to be healed of their infirmities. But he would withdraw to the desert and pray.
> (Luke 5:15–16; cf. Mark 1:35)

The competing interests that pull us away from moments of silent searching for God will almost certainly be less weighty than healing the sick or feeding the multitudes. They will not, however, be less difficult for us to resist. Perhaps this was the reason God so often physically removed his servants from the hustle and bustle of their regular lives to place them in the solitude of the wilderness. Perhaps there they would find fewer voices competing for their attention and be able to discern the one voice they so desperately needed to hear.

Be Prepared to Struggle

The Scriptures teach us that we may be better able to hear God's voice when we are in the wilderness. At the same time, though, we should steel ourselves to the fact that it is in the wilderness that we are most likely to face hardship and privation. This is true in a literal sense: If we retreat to a cabin in the woods or to a hospice for those on a spiritual pilgrimage, we will have to set aside certain "earthly delights" to do so. We may miss the big game on television or a dinner with friends. We may have to set aside work that needs to be done or chores that clamor for our attention. There are certain sacrifices that our "wilderness" experiences will demand. But there is also a more spiritual sort of hardship we may have to endure. Our times alone with God can be our most desperate.

In a study on the search for an elusive God, it is not surprising that we've crossed paths several times with Psalm 42 and its familiar opening line, "As the deer pants for streams of water, so my soul pants for you, O God." More than any other emotion, it is loneliness that marks the plight of the psalmist. The psalmist remembers with fondness the way he *used to* lead the throng in procession (v. 5), but now he's left only to wonder: "When shall I again appear before God?" (v. 3). A song about God is all that's left to the psalmist as he prays alone through the night (v. 9), and he must comfort his own soul with the hope that he will once again have opportunity to praise him (vv. 5, 11; 43:5).

Without the dull background noise of everyday life to distract us, questions and doubts whose depths we had never plumbed before may speak out more forcefully in our hearts. Guilt and uncertainty can tempt us away from God in the same way the tempter plied his trade against the Messiah when he was weak and hungry in the desert. Time spent alone and in silence before God can strip away what is extraneous and leave us exposed in God's presence. This is both the hope and the fear of seekers in the hands of an elusive God.

8

Seeking God in Doubt

It was for nothing that I kept my heart clean,
  and washed my hands in innocence.
For I have been stricken every day,
  and punished every morning.
        (Ps 73:13–14)

Losing Hope

IN MY PART OF THE WORLD (the humble city of Birmingham, Alabama), there's a place for those matters of moderate importance like religion and politics, so long as they don't interfere with things that are truly fundamental. Like football. Specifically, college football.

As a diehard Red Sox fan, I can attest to the intensity of the rivalry between the Sox and that team of modest import in a prior century still reputed to play in the Bronx. As a devotee of Auburn football, however, I can also attest that the antipathy between the Red Sox and Yankees is hardly more than a mild kerfuffle over the placement of a dessert fork when compared to the primeval hostility that exists between Auburn and Alabama. When the Yankees lose to the Sox, their fans retire peacefully to the company of other Yankees fans who commiserate with their feelings of disappointment. The same is true for those who pour their hearts out for the boys at Fenway.

But when Auburn or Alabama loses, the next day—and the day after and a year's worth of days after that—are far less pleasant. Half the office or class or worship service may share feelings of mutual disappointment, but the other half circles like vultures, grinning at their opponents' recent demise, ready to pick at the scraps.

Such is what makes the stakes so high at any particular college football game. On a long enough timeline, there will always come that moment when your team is playing against your biggest rival and the score has moved decidedly against your favor. "That's alright," you reassure yourself, "we always wait to the last moment to pull it out." But as the seconds keep ticking away, your mind eventually begins to weigh the "points behind" over against the "time to go." At a certain point, that feeling begins to creep in: "I don't know if we can do this or not. I don't really think we can." It's at this moment that we experience a certain pang in our hearts. An empty feeling. A sickening feeling. What we are feeling is *doubt*.

Doubt holds a unique place in our psyche because it weds both the *intellectual* part of our makeup—the part that calculates the spread between time left and points behind—and the *emotional* part—the growing dread at the disappointment that comes with losing. Doubt stands on the knife's edge between hope (that victory is possible) and resignation (that defeat is certain).

But what is doubt over something as silly as a sporting event when compared to *real* doubt—doubt that matters? True doubt comes when there is something vital on the line. This is the doubt we experience when a loved one is losing a battle with cancer, when hope for remission wanes, and we face the possibility that healing may not come after all. This is the doubt we experience when disaster strikes a place where your kids are supposed to be—the school they attend, the route they drive, the store where they work. There comes that moment when others have heard that their kids are safe, but no news has made it to you—that moment when hope for a call saying all is well turns to fear that another sort of call might arrive instead.

Spiritual Doubt

Though it may not share in the same kind of immediacy as these examples, spiritual doubt has an urgency and intensity all of its own. When the dam of our beliefs seems ready to collapse under the rising waters of our unanswered questions, a species of doubt can form that strikes at the deepest parts of who we are. Compounding this problem is the fact that we often add a layer of guilt to our feelings of doubt. And why not? There are, after all, a great many passages in the Bible that take a dim view of doubting. When Peter faltered on the waters of the Sea of Galilee, Jesus' response wasn't exactly a word of encouragement: "You of little faith, why did you doubt?" (Matt 14:31). He offered a similar rebuke to the pair of confused disciples he found walking on the road to Emmaus: "Why are you frightened, and why do doubts arise in your hearts?" (Luke 24:38). And consider what James had to say on the matter:

> If any of you lacks wisdom, let them ask God, who gives generously to all without reprimanding, and it will be given to them. But let them ask in faith *with no doubting*, because the one who doubts is like a wave of the sea that is driven and tossed by the wind—that sort of person should not expect to receive anything from the Lord. He is double-minded, unstable in all his ways!
>
> (Jas 1:5–8)

Double-minded, unstable, wind-tossed, and excluded from the Lord's gifts—that should just about settle it.

While I love the book of James—truthfully, it may be my favorite New Testament book—we should not regard the author's admonitions here as the *only* thing the Bible has to say about doubt. Indeed, before we move on to the rest of Scripture, we ought to note that James, much like the Old Testament prophets, often uses hyperbole—exaggerating for effect to get his message across (cf. Amos 4:1–2; 5:21; 8:2; 9:1–4; Jas 3:7–8; 4:4, 9; 5:1, 5). The Lord's brother isn't one for half-measures when he is trying to drive home a particular point. But the truth is that the pages of Scripture are filled with people who struggle with doubt. Indeed, the famous "Hall of Faith" in Hebrews 11 could easily be paired with a corresponding "Hall of Faltering" filled with nearly the same roster of characters: Abraham, Jacob, Moses, Joshua, Gideon, David, Elijah, Zechariah, John the Baptist, Peter, Thomas—not to mention Jesus himself.

Doubts Concerning God's Greatness

As we dig deeper into the lives of these figures, we see that spiritual doubt actually takes on different forms. At times, doubt swirls around God's *greatness*. Here, the questions revolve around whether what God has promised is so great that even he can't pull it off.

It was this sort of doubt that Abraham and Sarah wrestled with: Could God really provide them a son at their advanced age? This was what prompted Sarah to propose and Abraham to accept the idea of producing an heir through Sarah's maidservant Hagar (Gen 16). It was what led both of them on different occasions to laugh derisively at God's explicit promise that Sarah would bear a son (Abraham in Gen 17; Sarah in Gen 18).

It was ultimately doubt over God's greatness that led Moses to object so strenuously against God's call for him to go to Pharaoh (Exod 3–4). While Moses' first protested over his own inadequacy—"Who am I that I should go to Pharaoh?"—he quickly moved on to questioning *God's* abilities. His question, "What is your name?" is a loaded one. As we saw above, "name" in Hebrew often has to do with a person's reputation. God had answered Moses' concern about who *Moses* was by saying he himself would be with him. But Moses' reply to this was essentially to say, "That's great, but who are *you*? What's your reputation? What have you done?"[1] This is what prompted God to respond so forcefully with the rebuke, "I AM WHO I AM!" In time, it would not only be Moses but Moses' followers, the Israelites, who doubted God's greatness. Time and again, they questioned whether God could really provide food and water in the wilderness, whether he could really protect them from enemies in the wilderness and enemies in the promised land. Peter's doubts in his abortive attempt to walk on the sea fall into this same category (Matt 14). With the winds and the waves buffeting on every side, could Jesus truly impart to Peter the ability to join him on the water?

Doubts Concerning God's Goodness

As difficult as doubts concerning God's greatness may be, harder still are the doubts that arise concerning God's *goodness*. These are the doubts that wrestle not with whether God *can* do something, but whether he *will*. It is knowing God has the power to act and yet seeing him refuse to do so that plants questions in our hearts about God's character. This is the dilemma experienced by the writer of Psalm 10. From the outset, he asks:

> Why, O Lord, do you stand far off,
>   and hide yourself in times of trouble?
>
>   (v. 1)

Especially troubling for the psalmist is the fact that bad people, people he labels repeatedly as "the wicked," not only trample the poor on their way to success but boast in their rejection of God:

> The wicked with their turned up noses say God will not seek them out;[2]
> All their thoughts are "There is no God."
>
> (v. 4)

> They think in their hearts, "God has forgotten,
> he has hidden his face; he will never see."
>
> (v. 11)

The psalmist's struggle comes to a head in verses 12–13:

> Rise up, O Lord! O God, raise your hand!
> Do not forget the oppressed!
> Why should the wicked renounce God,
> saying in their hearts you won't seek them out?

You can see the psalmist's dilemma: When he calls on God to "rise up," when he asks why the wicked are allowed to renounce God, he is admitting that what the wicked people are saying *is* correct: God *has* forgotten. He *has* hidden his face. He *doesn't* see. Or if he does see, then it may be even worse. Perhaps God sees *but just doesn't care*.

We see the same sort of struggle in the tear-stained pages of the book of Jeremiah. Jeremiah struggles profoundly with the goodness of God. The prophet doesn't doubt for an instant that God is powerful. After all, Jeremiah believes it is God himself who has roused the Babylonian Empire to execute judgment on his people. What Jeremiah struggles to believe is that God is good, that God can be merciful, that God can forgive. In Jeremiah 4:10, he accuses God of deceiving the people into imagining their terrible fate can be avoided: "Ah, my Lord YHWH, surely you have utterly deceived this people and Jerusalem, saying, 'You shall have peace,' while the sword is at the throat!" In 12:1, he echoes the sentiments of Job as he laments:

> You will be in the right, O Lord,
> if I bring a case against you,
> yet judgments I shall speak against you.
> Why does the way of the wicked prosper?
> All the workers of treachery are at ease!

A few chapters later, he says to God, "You are to me like a deceitful stream, like waters that cannot be relied upon" (15:18). Doomed to see only God's judgment and not his mercy, Jeremiah laments over his call in a way no other prophet does:

> You seduced me, O Lord, and I was seduced;
> > you overpowered me, and you prevailed.
> I have become a laughingstock all day long;
> > everyone jeers at me.
>
> > > (20:7)

The language of seduction and overpowering here is some of the most powerful and, indeed, shocking in all of Scripture as it evokes images of sexual assault.[3] Jeremiah would resign his call if he could (v. 9), but since he can't, he wishes simply that he had never been born (vv. 14–18).

It is worth taking a moment to consider the way two of humanity's greatest artists, Michelangelo and Rembrandt, portray Jeremiah. Jeremiah is often called the "weeping prophet," but there are no tears in either of these artists' works. In both, Jeremiah is a man beyond tears, worn out from his futile preaching, cursed to see the destruction of his own people. These are depictions of spiritual exhaustion born out of a lifetime of doubt and struggle. Those who struggle with spiritual doubt may see their reflection in the prophet's own sorrowful countenance. Indeed, Michelangelo's Jeremiah is almost certainly a self-portrait. The great artist's lengthy bouts of depression are captured in Jeremiah's mournful gaze.

Most important of all among the biblical figures who struggled with doubt is Jesus' own long night of the soul. From the garden to the cross, Jesus experienced moments of profound spiritual doubt. Importantly, that doubt centered on the Father's goodness. In the late hours of the night, after their Passover meal had come to a close, Jesus and his disciples made their way to a place called Gethsemane. Mark's Gospel tells us what happened next:

> He said to his disciples, "Sit here while I pray." And he took with him Peter and James and John, and he began to be very distressed and troubled. He said to them, "My soul is very sorrowful, even to death. Remain here and keep watch." Going a little farther, he fell upon the ground and prayed that, if it were possible, the hour might pass from him. And he

said, "Abba, Father, all things are possible for you; take this cup from me; but not what I want but what you want."
(Mark 14:32b–36)

Most readers tend to focus only on the concluding line of Jesus' prayer, "Not what I want but what you want." These words, however, form only the final concession of his petition. What Jesus truly wanted is found rather in Mark's summarizing statement: "He prayed that, if it were possible, the hour might pass from him." Jesus was *willing* to go through with the cross; what Jesus *wanted*, however, was for the Father to deliver him from it.

We find confirmation of this in Jesus' seemingly cryptic words, "Take this cup from me." In three of the four Gospels, Jesus' death on the cross occurs immediately after he drinks the old wine that is offered to him:

> And immediately, one ran from him and took a sponge and filled it with sour wine and put it on a stick and gave it to him to drink. But the others said, "Wait, let's see if Elijah will come and save him." *Then Jesus, crying out again with a loud voice, yielded up his spirit.*
> (Matt 27:48–50)

> Then someone ran and filled a sponge with sour wine and put it on a stick and gave it to drink, saying, "Wait, let's see if Elijah will come to take him down." *Then Jesus uttered a loud cry and breathed his last.*
> (Mark 15:36–37)

> After this, Jesus, knowing that all was finished, in order that the scripture might be fulfilled, said, "I thirst." A jar full of sour wine was sitting there, so a sponge full of the sour wine was placed upon hyssop and held up to his mouth. When he had received the wine, Jesus said, "It is finished." *Then, bowing his head, he gave up his spirit.*
> (John 19:28–30)

It is this connection between Jesus' drinking the wine and "breathing his last" that tells us what he meant when he prayed, "Remove this *cup* from me." The cup in this context refers metonymically to Jesus' death. His prayer is that the Father might deliver him from the terrible death that awaited him. This is the same cup that Jesus warned James and John about when they asked for prime seats in the kingdom to come: "Are you able to drink the cup that I am about to drink?" (Matt 20:22; Mark 10:38).

Not to be missed is the fact that Jesus' prayer that the Father remove the cup from him—his prayer that he not be forced to go through the cross—is prefaced by these words: "Abba, Father, *all things* are possible for you" (Mark 14:36). The foundation of Jesus' prayer is the fact that the Father *could* remove his Son from the terrible suffering that would ensue. He could remove him if he would only *choose* to do so. But the Father would not choose to do so. And thus, we arrive at Jesus' heart-wrenching cry on the cross, "My God, my God, *why* have you forsaken me?" There is no question of God's power in this moment. God surely could have relieved Jesus' sufferings and rescued him from him from his executioners—if he had wanted to. But God had not. This is what leads to that profound question, "Why?" Jesus does not lament, "O that you had the power to rescue me!" He knows God has that power and doesn't understand why he would not come to his aid.

It's interesting to note that while there are seven famous sayings of Jesus on the cross, Mark records only one, the cry of abandonment that centers on the word "Why?" In Mark, Jesus' death is not accompanied by words like "Into your hands I commit my spirit" or "It is finished." There is only this: "Then Jesus uttered a loud cry and breathed his last" (Mark 15:37). More clearly than the other Gospels, Mark gives us a full view of the Messiah's humanity. It is a tender picture, a moving picture of the doubt even the Son of God endured. No wonder the author of Hebrews could say that we do not have a high priest who cannot sympathize with us: "He has been tempted in all respects just as we are, yet without sin" (Heb 4:15).

Doubt Is Not a Sin

The doubts Jesus expressed in the hours leading up to the cross are of inestimable importance for his would-be followers. In the first place, Jesus' doubts confirm for us that *doubt is not a sin*. While nearly every New Testament writer wrestles in one way or another with the relationship between Jesus' humanity and his divinity, one truth that remains unchallenged is the belief that Jesus lived a sinless life. Jesus could hunger, thirst, sleep, learn, and die—all things that vividly illustrate the fullness of the Messiah's humanity —but unlike any other human, Jesus did not sin. If Jesus experienced moments of doubt, then doubt in and of itself must not be sinful.

Jesus' doubts also confirm for us that even doubts centered on God's goodness rather than his greatness aren't sinful. Truthfully, this is the aspect of doubt that is the most difficult to deal with. The vast majority of human beings—past and present—have believed instinctively that God exists and that God is powerful. Scripture insists that it is only with considerable effort that they do otherwise, given the din of creation's voice declaring these truths to be so (cf. Rom 1:19–20; Ps 8). But it is the very fact that we believe God is powerful that gives birth to our spiritual crises. If God is powerful, that is, if God *can* act, then why *doesn't* he? While it may be wrong to move from doubt to disbelief, doubt itself is not a sin, even when that doubt focuses on God's goodness.

The Way Out Is Through

If there is an additional lesson to be learned from Jesus' struggles with doubt, it is that the path forward is one that leads *through*, not around, doubt. Jesus didn't continue his journey to the cross because he had resolved his doubts. He went through this terrible torture *despite* his doubts. He believed the Father had it within his power to deliver him from the cross. He believed the Father's actions were by choice, not by necessity. And yet he chose to go through his suffering on the cross anyway. He lamented right up until his final death-embracing cry; he never stopped doubting. But even in the midst of these profound doubts, he lived up to the words of his prayer, "Not my will, but yours be done."

Seeking God in the Midst of Doubt

I am jealous of those who never struggle with spiritual doubt. Such has not been the experience of my walk of faith. I'm not going anywhere. I've been at this long enough to know that Christianity is true, and so I know there really isn't anywhere else *to* go. That doesn't make the hard moments any less hard, though. The only question is what to do about it. How do we seek an elusive God in the midst of doubt?

Shoulder the Burden for Others

There is a kind of intimacy in the Gospel accounts of Gethsemane that ought to give us pause as we approach them. The Son's pleas to the Father hallow the garden setting so entirely that, like Moses, we should be careful as we approach this holy ground. At the same time, we shouldn't forget that even in the garden, a third party was present—in spirit if not physically. *We* were there. Jesus went through with the cross not only because he believed it was the Father's will, but also because he knew it had to be done on our behalf. John's Gospel captures this aspect of Jesus' death with particular clarity:

> I am the good shepherd; *the good shepherd lays down his life for the sheep.*
> (John 10:11)

> I am the good shepherd, and I know my own and my own know me, just as the Father knows me and I know the Father, and *I lay down my life for the sheep.*
> (John 10:14–15)

> Greater love than this has no one, *that one lay down one's life for one's friends.*
> (John 15:13)

> Before the festival of the Passover, Jesus knew that his hour had come to depart from this world to the Father. Having loved his own who were in the world, *he loved them to the end.*
> (John 13:1)

These passages tell us that even in the midst of extraordinary doubt, Jesus managed to press on *for the sake of others around him.*

It is not just the Messiah who has others who depend on him. Though in one sense our spiritual journey is ours alone, there are those around us who may be deeply affected by it. On one occasion in the Gospels, Jesus' disciples ask him who is greatest in the kingdom of heaven (Matt 18:1–6; cf. Mark 9:42; Luke 17:2). Calling a child over, Jesus insists, "The one who humbles himself like this child will be the greatest in the kingdom of heaven" (Matt 18:4). Then he adds a quite sobering coda:

> The one who receives this child in my name receives me. *But the one who causes one of these little ones who believe in me to stumble,* it would be better for that one to have a great millstone hung around his neck and to be drowned in the depths of the sea.
> (v. 6)

Here, Jesus envisions the possibility that one person's faults might shipwreck another person's faith. Jesus is certainly not alone in this regard. Paul warns his Roman readers not to put a "stumbling block" in front of others who may be struggling in their faith (Rom 14:13). Paul's use of the noun *skandalon* ("stumbling block") aligns with Matthew's translation of Jesus' words using the verb *skandalizō* ("to cause to stumble"). Though Jesus originally spoke in Aramaic and Paul in Greek, they both have in mind the idea that we possess the ability to undermine the faith of other people. Paul uses similar language as he warns the believers at Corinth about abusing their liberty in Christ. He cautions, "See that this liberty of yours does not somehow become a hindrance to those who are weak," and goes so far as to say that this weak person, this "brother for whom Christ died," can be "destroyed" through our selfish actions (1 Cor 8:9–11).

It may be a difficult burden to bear, but it remains true that a great many people may be influenced by our own faith commitments. If we walk away—if we let our doubts get the best of us, if we move from doubt to despair, if we move from doubt to denial, if we finally give up on the faith—we will almost certainly take others with us in the process. But if we experience times of doubt—even profound, heart-wrenching doubts—and choose to continue our walk of faith, then we create a space for our spouses, children, grandchildren, and others to keep searching for God's presence in their own lives.

Follow in the Footsteps of Jesus

When faced with his most difficult moments of doubt, Jesus chose the course that took him *through* the challenges he faced. Even as his doubts concerning God's seeming absence lingered, Jesus set his face toward the cross and endured the worst the Romans could throw at him. As we noted above, Jesus did this, in part, for the sake of those whose faith depended on his fidelity. Jesus pressed on through doubt to serve those who needed him. There is a lesson for us here in Jesus' commitment to serve others.

In an earlier chapter, we considered the way worship and ritual can serve as "coaches" that urge us to keep moving even when we don't feel like it. Devotion to serving others—just as Jesus did—can serve the same function in our spiritual lives. Following in the footsteps of Jesus by acting as servants to others can keep us moving along a path of faith even when our hearts are ready to give up the journey.

There may be no more vivid example of this aspect of service than the life and letters of Mother Teresa. Though this servant to the poor of Calcutta was nearly always seen with a smile on her face and a sprightly and loving aspect to her demeanor, it's now clear that she suffered through decades of profound spiritual crisis. The extent of Teresa's wrestling with spiritual darkness was only discovered after her death with the publication of *Come Be My*

Light, a collection of letters to her superiors and confessors over the course of sixty-six years.[4] The sorts of doubts to which Mother Teresa confesses are heartbreaking—and all too familiar to those of us who have walked through a similar valley of the shadow of death. Writing to one trusted confidant in September of 1979, she insists:

> Jesus has a very special sort of love for you—for you are so totally His that you live—not you—but Jesus lives in you and through you He proves His love for the world. As for me—the silence and the emptiness is so great that I look and do not see, listen and do not hear.—The tongue moves but does not speak.[5]

The excruciating length of her spiritual suffering is evident in the fact that she had expressed similar thoughts a full two decades before:

> Lord, my God, who am I that You should forsake me? The child of your love—and now become as the most hated one—the one You have thrown away as unwanted—unloved. I call, I cling, I want—and there is no One to answer—no One on Whom I can cling, no, No One.—Alone.[6]

Similar doubts would persist all the way to her death in 1997.

The letters and confessions found in *Come Be My Light* were not intended by Mother Teresa to garner either public sympathy or acclaim. Her express wishes were that these private communications remain private and indeed be destroyed, but she was overruled by her ecclesiastical superiors. Nor were these items published by critics to somehow tarnish Teresa's extraordinary public standing. On the contrary, the Rev. Brian Kolodiejchuk, who assembled the works, was the very person who petitioned for her canonization as a saint and who gathered these correspondences to *support* her candidacy. Kolodiejchuk and the various ecclesiasts who refused to destroy Teresa's communications understood that ordinary Christians would derive great value from seeing how deeply she suffered and how determined she was to continue her life of service *despite* her great suffering. Mother Teresa's spiritual struggles do nothing to undermine her status as a hero of the faith. Quite the opposite: They vividly illustrate that the only way through some seasons of doubt may be to follow in the footsteps of Jesus' own life of service. It was Teresa's love for the poor and her devotion to serving them that kept her moving toward God even when the path ahead seemed its darkest.

Be Clear-Eyed About the Alternative

It's hardly fair that one disciple, Thomas, has the misfortune of being singled out with the epithet "Doubting." Thomas was hardly alone in struggling to believe Jesus had been raised from the dead; the other disciples were just as reticent to believe before they had their chance to lay eyes on the risen Christ. Perhaps Thomas should have taken the other disciples' word for it when they said, "We have seen the Lord." Perhaps he shouldn't have been quite so dramatic in saying, "Unless I see in his hands the mark of the nails and put my finger in the mark of the nails and put my hand in his side, I will not believe" (John 20:25).

In any case, Thomas doubted, and for a time, it seemed his doubts were well-founded. A full week went by between Thomas' declaration and Jesus' next appearance to the disciples. This time, Thomas was with them. As Jesus approached him, he was ready to take his skeptical disciple up on his challenge. He said to him, "Put your finger here and see my hands. Reach out your hand and put it in my side. Do not doubt but believe" (v. 27). Thomas, of course, did no such thing. Instead, he exclaimed, "My Lord and my God!" Of particular importance for us is what Jesus said to Thomas next: "Have you believed because you have seen me? *Blessed are those who have not seen and yet have come to believe*" (v. 29). With these words, Jesus expressed sympathy for *us*. Jesus himself acknowledged that belief would be difficult in generations to come. These are the same sentiments Peter expressed to the persecuted recipients of his first letter:

> Though you have not seen him, you love him. Though you do not see him now, you believe in him and rejoice with inexpressible and glorious joy, receiving the ultimate end of your faith, the salvation of your souls.
> (1 Pet 1:8–9)

A life of faith is almost always hard. It requires trusting in what cannot be fully seen. It requires hoping even in times of great darkness. It requires continuing to believe in the goodness of God even when God's creation seems so broken. Doubt is understandable, perhaps even unavoidable, but there is comfort in knowing that Jesus himself sympathizes with us as we struggle.

9

Seeking God in Suffering

I refuse! I would not live forever.
  Leave me alone, for my days are but a breath.
What is man that you make so much of him,
  that you set your heart upon him?
That you visit him every morning,
  think about him every moment?
Will you not just look away from me?
  Will you not loose your grip on me so I can swallow my spit?
    (Job 7:16–19)

Beautiful but Broken

IN WHAT IS LIKELY ERNEST HEMINGWAY'S most famous line, Robert Jordan, the protagonist of *For Whom the Bell Tolls*, insists, "The world is a fine place and worth the fighting for." That Jordan says these words a few moments *after* his horse had fallen on him and shattered his leg and a few moments *before* the bell would finally toll for him captures something of the dilemma we face in creation. The world is a beautiful place, but all of the Bible's creation traditions insist that same world is not *now* the way it ought to be.

In poetic creation accounts like Psalms 74:12–17 and 89:6–12, God's creative work is accomplished by battling against and subduing sea and dragon:

> You broke the sea by your might;
>> you shattered the heads of the dragons in the waters,
> you crushed the heads of Leviathan.
>
>> (Ps 74:13–14a)
>
> You rule the raging of the sea;
>> when its waves rise, you still them.
> You crushed Rahab like a carcass;
>> you scattered your enemies with your mighty arm.
>
>> (Ps 89:9–10)

But the sea and the dragon are always poised to break out again, a point particularly evident in the fact that both Psalms 74 and 89 are psalms of lament. In the former, the nation's temple has been destroyed and still lies in ruins (74:1–12). In the latter, it is the Davidic king who has suffered profound rejection and defeat (89:40–53). God may have won his victory over the forces of chaos in the days of old, but that same chaos had broken out again in the lifetime of the psalmists.

Such was the case, too, for the Israelites who suffered under Pharaoh's lash. The nation had descended from the promise of freedom in Canaan to the curse of slavery in Egypt, and so what God had accomplished at creation he must do again in the exodus:

> Awake, awake, clothe yourself with strength,
>> O arm of the Lord!
> Awake, as in days of old,
>> the generations of old!
> Was it not you who hacked Rahab in pieces,
>> who pierced the dragon?
> Was it not you who dried up the sea,
>> the waters of the great deep;
> who made the depths of the sea a way
>> for the redeemed to cross over?
>
>> (Isa 51:9–10)

And what God did in the exodus, he must do yet once more in the age to come:

> *On that day*, the Lord with his hard and great and strong sword will punish Leviathan the fleeing serpent, Leviathan the twisting serpent, and he will kill the dragon that is in the sea.
>
>> (Isa 27:1)

The prose accounts of creation tell a similar story. In Genesis 1, the primordial waters and darkness of verse 2 are controlled by God's creative work, but they are not removed entirely. As in the passages above, the waters and darkness are always there, lurking, ready to break out all over again and overwhelm us. In Genesis 2–3, it is our own sinfulness that brings a curse upon creation, shifting it from ally to enemy and turning cheerful tending inside the garden into ceaseless toil outside of it.

Even the apostle Paul echoes this element of creation in a moving passage in his letter to the Romans:

> For the eagerly awaiting creation waits earnestly for the revelation of the sons of God. For the creation was subjected to futility, not willingly, but by the will of the one who subjected it, in hope that the creation would one day be freed from its bondage to corruption and into the freedom of the glory of the children of God. We know that all of creation groans and suffers together up till now, not alone, but with us, those who share the first fruits of the Spirit, we who ourselves groan as we eagerly await the adoption, the release of our bodies.
>
> (Rom 8:19–23)

Creation languishes under the effects of the curse. Like God's children, it, too, longs for the day when redemption becomes a reality. Until then, it remains broken, desperate for repair.

God and the Satan

Unfortunately, we are not only spectators, observing the brokenness of the world, but participants in its travails. We suffer alongside creation, and it is often this suffering—both our own and that of creation—that produces our most profound feelings of doubt. Nowhere is this seen more vividly than in the famous account of the suffering of Job.

After its memorable opening line, "There once was a man from the land of Uz," the book of Job goes on to describe the extraordinary character of the book's namesake. Job, we are told, was the proud father of seven sons and three daughters, a man of wealth and prestige, a figure who stood out as "the greatest man in the East." But Job was not only a great man; he was also a good man. Indeed, both the narrator and God himself (twice!) describe Job as "blameless and upright, one who fears God and turns away from evil" (cf. 1:1, 8; 2:3). He's a man so righteous that he even offers "just in case" sacrifices on behalf of his children. Who knows, he wonders, whether they might have sinned and cursed God in their hearts (1:8).

Job's outstanding character remains the focus of the story as the scene shifts from earth to heaven. An ominous note is struck, though, when the "sons of God" present themselves and God addresses one in particular, a character called "the Satan."[1] While Satan takes on a larger role in the New Testament, where he is variously referred to as Satan, the devil, or just "the enemy," he appears by name only three times in the Hebrew Bible. On one occasion, he is said to incite David to take a census (1 Chr 21:1).[2] On another, he charges that a certain Joshua is unfit to serve as high priest because he had been among the exiles to Babylon (Zech 3:1–2). And then there is his appearance in Job 1–2. Particularly in these last two contexts, the Satan's role appears to be that of, for want of a better expression, "devil's advocate." What God suggests, it is the Satan's job to challenge. Caught in the middle of this rhetorical tug-of-war between God and the Satan is innocent Job.

With God's question to the Satan —"Have you considered my servant Job?"—a series of events begins to unfold that will ultimately rob Job of nearly everything he has. For an honest reader, the twenty or so verses that narrate Job's fall are among the most challenging in the Bible. Truthfully, it isn't Job's suffering that makes the passage so hard. It is rather the role that God plays in his suffering. Why does God bring up Job to the Satan in the first place? Doesn't he know this would lead to tragedy for Job? How could God so casually say, "Everything he has is in your hands," when that "everything" includes the lives of Job's ten children, his many servants, and untold numbers of animals? What sort of God could be "incited" against his favorite servant just by the Satan's prodding? And what sort of God would "destroy" that servant "for nothing" (cf. Job 2:3)? How could God allow the Satan to wrack Job with pain and suffering *just to win a bet*?

These aren't easy questions. Indeed, they raise issues so difficult that our faith in God might prompt us to look away from them altogether. Believing what we believe about God, knowing what we know about God, these sorts of questions can seem too dangerous for us to look squarely in the eye. Better to pawn the blame off on the Satan or to cast Job and his children as somehow sinfully deserving their suffering. While these may be easier options, a moment's pause over God's part in the story proves them to be inadequate.

The Genre of the Book of Job

The challenges raised by God's actions in Job are alleviated somewhat if we take a moment to consider the genre of the book. While I recognize others will take a different view, it is my contention that though there may well have been a historical *figure* named Job who suffered greatly, the *book* of Job is a quite stylized retelling of Job's story.[3] Although *parable* would not be the precise word to describe the genre of the book, Job does share many features of the sorts of parables that Jesus told.

Opening Line

One example of the parable-like language in the book is found in its opening line: "There was a man in the land of Uz." If this language sounds familiar, it's for good reason; Jesus begins many of his parables in the same fashion. The parable of the good Samaritan, for example, begins with "A certain man was going down from Jerusalem . . . " (Luke 10:30), the parable of the prodigal son with "A certain man had two sons . . . " (Luke 15:11), and the parable of the wicked tenants with "A certain man had a vineyard . . ." (Luke 20:9). Interestingly, the opening words of the Septuagint's Greek translation of Job, *anthropos tis*, are identical to those found in Luke's Greek rendering of Jesus' parables; these stories begin with the same language because they share the same genre.

Access to the Divine Realm

Much like the parable of the rich man and Lazarus, the book of Job gives us access to the divine realm that is difficult to explain. It isn't a matter of whether God could interact with humanity; while some biblical scholars and theologians might have an issue with such things, I don't count myself among them. What's at issue in Job is rather the book's access to the heavenly scenes where God convenes and converses with his divine court. We are never told just how the author might be privy to such an audience; certainly no divine word or heavenly vision is mentioned. This is especially relevant in Job where a key aspect of the book lies in Job's *not* knowing the source of his sufferings but nonetheless remaining faithful.

Stylized Language

A careful reader of Job will notice how often the book's language falls into stylized and repetitive patterns. This is not to criticize this great work, of course; few books can contend with the literary artistry of Job. It is merely to point out that certain elements of the book's language seem unlikely to be straightforward historical reporting. Although they arrive separately and offer their reports individually, each one of the four messengers who come to inform Job of the loss of his animals, servants, and children concludes his message with the identical words, "I alone have escaped to tell you" (Hebrew: *wā'immāltâ raq 'ănî ləbaddî ləhaggîd lāk*). To this we might add the virtually identical language used to describe the arrival of the sons of God (1:6–7; 2:1–2), the divine question concerning Job's righteousness (1:8; 2:3), the Satan's explanation for that righteousness (1:9–11; 2:4–5), and the divine permission for harm given to the Satan (1:12; 2:6). This repetitive language sounds like nothing so much as the stylized language of Jesus' parables. We hear echoes of it in the repetitive cadence of the fate of the seed in the parable of the sower (Matt 13:3–9; Mark 4:3–9; Luke 8:5–8), the responses of the priest, Levite, and Samaritan who encounter the robbed and beaten man on the road to Jericho in the parable of the good Samaritan (Luke 10:31–33), and the recovery of the lost sheep, the lost coin, and the prodigal son (Luke 15).

The Poetic Dialogues

Though not specifically a feature of parables, the poetic language of Job 3:1–42:6 can hardly be overlooked. Whatever one's view of the historicity of Job, it seems difficult to believe that Job, his three "friends," Elihu, and God himself would spend nearly forty chapters of the book responding back and forth to one another in some of the most elevated and difficult poetry in the entire Hebrew Bible. One might just as well imagine a person on their deathbed arguing back and forth with a pastor in iambic pentameter.

Hyperbole

A key element of many parables is hyperbole, the literary device of exaggerating for effect. In the three parables noted above from Luke 15, for example, we find a shepherd who abandons his ninety-nine sheep to go searching for the one sheep that is lost, a woman who ransacks her house in search of a coin of only modest value, and a father who runs to greet the return of a son who had abandoned him. Each of these parables dramatically emphasizes the foolishness of the shepherd, woman, and father and the lesser worth of the sheep, coin, and son to highlight God's reckless pursuit of wayward individuals like ourselves.

The book of Job is filled with this sort of hyperbolic language. Job is not just wealthy, he is "the greatest man in the east" (1:3). He's not just a good man, but "upright, blameless, one who fears God and turns away from evil" (1:1, 8; 2:3). Job doesn't just experience difficulty; he suffers like almost no other. He loses every possession and all of his children in the span of just a few moments. He loses his own health to the point that he is reduced to sitting on an ash heap and scraping himself with a broken piece of pottery (2:8).

Clearly Didactic

Finally, parables are overtly didactic. They are thought experiments that force us to explore some aspect of faith or practice. The parables mentioned in the preceding paragraph are meant to make us consider the depths of the Father's love for us and the heights of our unworthiness. With the parable of the good Samaritan, Jesus prods us to consider not who our neighbor is (the lawyer's question) but *to whom we should be a neighbor*. The book of Job clearly falls into this category as well. This is not a book content merely to narrate the twists and turns of some historical event in the life of Israel. This is a book whose overarching purpose is to force us to consider something far more profound. What, then, is the lesson the book of Job intends to teach? What thought experiment does it challenge us to consider? Here, I beg the reader's indulgence as I know my answer may seem needlessly provocative. I trust that in the end it won't be, but it may take us a moment to get there. It is my contention that the book of Job pushes us to consider just this: *What would we do if God were to act outrageously?*

What Would You Do?

On a long enough timeline, I do not believe God acts outrageously. When that day comes when we no longer see "through a glass darkly but face to face" (1 Cor 13:12), I trust that we will understand why the world is the way it is and why God has acted the way he has. But in the here and now, on this side of the veil, God's actions—and his inactions—certainly do seem outrageous. No one was quicker to recognize this than the biblical authors themselves. Consider the words of just this handful of psalmists:

> Why, O Lord, do you stand far off,
> and hide yourself in times of trouble?
>
> (Ps 10:1)

> How long, O Lord, will you forget me forever?
> How long will you hide your face from me?
>
> (Ps 13:1)

> My God, my God, why have you forsaken me?
> Why so far from delivering me, from the words of my crying out!
>
> (Ps 22:1)

> For your sake we are being killed all day long;
> we are counted as sheep for slaughtering.
> Awake! Why do you sleep, O Lord?
> Wake up! Do not reject us forever.
> Why do you hide your face,
> and forget our misery and oppression?
>
> (Ps 44:22–24)

Note the recurring questions in these lines—Why? How long?—and the accusations that accompany them: You stand far away. You hide yourself in times of trouble. You hide your face. You've forgotten me. You've forsaken me. You sleep. You forget our affliction. We are being killed because of you.

These sentiments could be multiplied many times over just from the Psalter. But these are not questions born out of blasphemy or disbelief. They arise from hearts that genuinely do not understand why God is acting the way he is or refusing to act when they believe he should. The psalmists express confidence that, in time, God will act justly; after all, every psalm of lament save one (Ps 88) eventually turns to praise. But in that moment, in the depths of the psalmists' suffering, God *appears* to be acting outrageously, and they turn to him to ask why. What these psalms do in brief the book of Job does at length. Over the course of forty-two difficult chapters, it asks us to consider for ourselves the terrible question of what we would do if God *were* to act this way.

"You Have Not Spoken Rightly"

The book of Job goes out of its way to cast God's actions in it as outrageous. Beyond the questions raised above concerning God's part in the commencement of Job's suffering, we must also contend with the book's concluding verses, 42:7–17. The longest part of the book, chapters 3–29, consists of Job's arguments or "dialogues" with Eliphaz, Bildad, and Zophar, the friends who come ostensibly to comfort him but ultimately serve as his antagonists. While Job forcefully defends his innocence and pleads with God for an audience, his three "comforters" are equally dogmatic in their insistence that Job's suffering can only result from his guilt. Eliphaz argues:

> Remember now, who that was innocent has perished?
>   And where have the righteous been cut off?
> As I have seen, those who plow iniquity
>   and sow trouble reap it.
>   (Job 4:7–8)

Bildad adds:

> Does God pervert justice?
>   Does the Almighty pervert what is right?
> If your children sinned against him,
>   then he delivered them over to their offence.
>   (Job 8:3–4)

Zophar chimes in:

> Know that God has actually overlooked many of your sins!
>   (Job 11:6)

Throughout these dialogues, Job's interlocutors insist on God's justice while Job harshly criticizes it. If God is just, then he must surely side with the friends in this debate. *And yet he does not.* With the poetic portion of the book complete, the prose epilogue begins in 42:7 with these words:

> And it happened after the LORD had spoken these words to Job, that the LORD said to Eliphaz the Temanite, "My anger burns *against you and your two friends*, for you have not spoken rightly about me *as my servant Job has*."

Again, note carefully what God says to Eliphaz: "*You* have not spoken rightly about me, *as my servant Job has.*" Job questioned God's justice, Eliphaz and his friends defended it, but God sides with Job. This pattern continues in God's subsequent instructions to Eliphaz in verse 8:

> Now, take for yourself seven bulls and seven rams, and go to my servant Job, and offer up for yourselves a burnt offering. My servant Job will pray for you.

So great is the offence of Job's antagonists that they require his intercession. The defenders of God's justice require prayer and sacrifice *from Job*, their opponent. Of particular importance is the divine explanation for *why* Job's intercession is required. God repeats again his earlier reason, "For you have not spoken rightly concerning me, as my servant Job has."

To this first reason, however, God adds another. Most translations, including the NRSVue, ESV, and NIV, render this additional explanation as, "For I will accept his prayer not to deal with you according to your folly." A glance at the translation in the King James Version—"lest I deal with you *after your* folly"—raises a question, though. Note here that certain words in the clause are set in italics; this is the convention used in the KJV not to mark emphasis but rather to indicate a *paraphrase* that departs from the underlying Hebrew. The same phrase is also marked in this fashion in the NASB: "So that I may not do with you *according to your* folly." At issue here is the fact that the words "according to your" simply do not appear in the Hebrew text. Though most translations hesitate to translate the text as it stands, the actual Hebrew in verse 8b is better rendered as "lest I deal foolishly with you" or "lest I do something foolish to you." The Hebrew word *nəbālâ*, "folly" or "foolishness," is applied to *God's* actions, not those of the friends. The divine concession that lingers in the wake of this warning is obvious: Lest I deal foolishly with you . . . *as I did with Job.*

Divine Restitution

One last item to consider has to do with the divine restitution made to Job. We could read the closing verses of the book as a sort of "and they all lived happily ever after" ending to the story. Of course, this would not be entirely accurate since having ten new children could hardly compensate for the lost lives of Job's earlier children. More interesting, though, is the implication hinted at in the words, "And the LORD gave Job twice as much as he had before" (42:10). Double restitution is what the law requires when someone takes something from a person *unlawfully*:

> If the stolen item is indeed found alive in his possession—whether ox or donkey or sheep—he shall restore double.
> (Exod 22:4)

> If a person gives to their neighbor money or goods to keep, and they are stolen from the neighbor's house, if the thief is found, he shall restore double.
> (Exod 22:7)

> In any matter of criminal action involving an ox or donkey or sheep or garment or any other lost property concerning which a person says, "This is it!" the case of both parties shall come before God, and the one whom God declares guilty shall restore double to their neighbor.
> (Exod 22:9)

Of course, one might object, "But how could God possibly take something unlawfully?" But note what even the book of Job itself says concerning Job's recovery:

> All his brothers and sisters and former acquaintances came to Job, and they ate bread with him in his house, and they showed sympathy to him and comforted him *over all the evil that the* L<small>ORD</small> *had brought upon him*.
> (Job 42:11)

Here, the book is explicit in mentioning the wrong that was done to Job. The book goes out of its way to do so.

Seeking God in Suffering

While we can hardly avoid reading Scripture through our own theological lenses, Scripture itself urges us to read the book of Job in a new way. It means to challenge us, to force us to consider what our hearts don't want to consider: What would we do if God *were* to act outrageously? And if Job pushes us to consider this soul-searching question, it would be a terrible mistake not to consider the answers the book gives as well. As the quintessential book about suffering, the lessons of Job can only help us as we seek God during our own times of suffering.

Praise

In the prose prologue of the book, Job responds to the loss of his family with a resolve so stoic it is difficult to comprehend: "Naked I came from my mother's belly, and naked shall I return there. The LORD gave and the LORD has taken away. May the name of the LORD be blessed."[4] Even after the loss of his own health, Job replies to his wife's urging to "curse God and die"[5] with a steadfast "Shall we accept good from God and not accept evil?" (2:10).

Athalya Brenner observes that Job's pious acceptance of his fate "is positively saintly." But she then asks, " Is it human as well?"[6] Job's later protests may suggest that his initial response reflects a certain state of denial. Whether this is the case or not, though, we shouldn't ignore the book's stipulation that there was nothing sinful in his statements. The narrator's response to Job's affirmations that he was born to die ("Naked I came from my mother's belly, and naked shall I return there"; 2:10) and that we should be as ready to accept evil from God as good ("Shall we accept good from God and not accept evil?"; 1:21) was to say, "In all this, Job did not sin, and he did not charge God with wrongdoing" (1:22).

If we *can* respond to suffering with words of praise like those Job uttered, then we should, by all means, do so. We certainly find encouragement to meet suffering with praise in many other places in the Bible. Most often, authors ask us to see suffering as times of strengthening and refining. James, for example, urges us to "consider it all joy, my brothers, when you face various trials, knowing that the testing of your faith produces endurance" (Jas 1:2–3). In a similar vein, Peter tells his readers:

> In this you rejoice, though now you must suffer various trials, in order that the testing of your faith—faith more precious than gold which, though perishable, is tested by fire—may be found to produce praise and glory and honor at the revelation of Jesus Christ.
> (1 Pet 1:6–7)

Other authors challenge us to look beyond our present circumstances to the reward that awaits us in the future. In the Sermon on the Mount, Jesus insists:

> Blessed are those who are persecuted for the sake of righteousness, for *theirs is the kingdom of heaven*. Blessed are you when they insult you and persecute you and say all manner of evil against you falsely for my sake. Rejoice and be glad, *for great is your reward in heaven*.
> (Matt 5:10–12a)

And the author of Hebrews tells us to look to Jesus' example on the cross when we suffer:

> Let us run with endurance the race that lies before us, fixing our eyes on Jesus, the founder and finisher of our faith, who *for the joy that was set before him endured the cross*, disregarding the shame, and sat down at the right hand of the throne of God.
> (Heb 12:1a–2)

As much as it lies within us, we should work to respond to suffering with praise. We *should* look to the example of Jesus, who cried out during his suffering but still committed his spirit to God with his final breath (Luke 23:46). We *should* recall the transitory nature of our present sufferings, knowing that the healing comfort of God's presence ultimately awaits us (Rev 21:4). We *should* consider the fact that God may be using our suffering to refine our character and produce a spiritual toughness that we lack. All of these are things we should do, but that doesn't mean they are the *only* things we should do.

Lament

Each one of us has a different gait to our spiritual walk, so it should be no surprise that we each respond differently to times of joy and times of suffering. For some, suffering creates no cognitive dissonance, no scars on the soul. I envy those sorts of people, even if I can't fully relate to the inner workings of their spiritual lives. I envy their ability to say *and mean* words of praise even in the midst of intense suffering. I take comfort, though, in the fact that praise isn't the only response to suffering that we find in the Scriptures. Sometimes before, sometimes after, sometimes intermixed with praise, we also find lament.

When the Satan strikes Job himself, he does so with a vengeance. Sores cover Job from the crown of his head to the soles of his feet, wracking his body with so much pain that he can only sit among the ashes, scraping his skin with a broken piece of pottery for relief. After a week of sitting in silence with his friends and with no end to his suffering in sight, Job finally cries out with words other than praise. Now, Job turns to words of curse and lament instead. Job offers bitter curses against the day of birth and the night of his conception (3:1–10), and he laments to God over his seemingly unending suffering (3:11–26).

When the many chapters of Job's laments finally come to an end, the Lord speaks to Job "out of the whirlwind" (38:1–39:30). The tone of this lengthy speech is so harsh that it is easy to conclude that God is disappointed with Job for speaking out at all. To put it bluntly, we might think God would prefer that Job just shut up. Job had worried all along that even if God were to give him an audience, God would only bully him into silence:

> If I summoned him, and he answered me,
> > I do not believe he would give ear to my voice.
> For he crushes me with a storm,
> > and multiplies my wounds for no reason.
> He will not let me catch my breath,
> > but fills me with bitterness.
> If it is a matter of strength, he is the strong one;
> > if a matter of justice, who can summon him for me?
> Though I am innocent, my own mouth will declare me guilty;
> > I am blameless, but my mouth will denounce me as perverse.
>
> > > > (9:16–20)

With God's litany of "Where were you?" and "Do you know?" questions in chapters 38–39, Job's fears seem to have been well-founded. After all, God never addresses the issue of justice; he speaks only about his power. But it is God's unjust exercise of power toward Job that lies at the heart of Job's laments. And so, duly chastened by the Lord's rebuke, Job gives up the fight. He responds to God's rehearsal of his great wisdom and power with words of surrender:

> I am too small; how can I reply to you?
> > I cover my mouth with my hand.
> I spoke once, but I will not answer again,
> > twice, but I will not continue.
>
> > > > (40:4–5)

If God's intention was to shut Job up, then he succeeded. With the lesson "Don't Complain to God" now firmly in place, the book could finally draw to a close. But there we face a problem: The book doesn't end with Job's surrender. Instead, God launches into another lengthy speech (40:6–41:34). Although the first divine speech could hardly have gone worse for Job, this second speech differs dramatically from the first. It begins with a call for Job to assume the bearing and aspect of a king:

> Deck yourself with pride and loftiness,
> > clothe yourself with majesty and splendor.
> Scatter your foes with the outburst of your anger,
> > look upon the arrogant and abase them.
> Look upon the arrogant and humble them,
> > and trample the wicked where they stand.
> Bury them all together in the dust,
> > hide their faces in obscurity.
>
> > (40:10–13)

We may be tempted to read these encouragements with a tone of divine irony or even sarcasm. Surely, it is laughable to imagine God would have to live up to his challenge: "Then even I will praise you, for your right hand would give you victory" (v. 14). But then there is the second part of this second speech.

After instructing Job to take on the mantle of a king, God next charges him to consider two mythical creatures, the Behemoth (40:15–24) and the Leviathan (41:1–34).[7] It is the Leviathan here that is of particular importance. As we saw above, the Leviathan does only one thing in Scripture: *It fights with God* (cf. Pss 74:13–14; 104:26; Isa 27:1).[8] This aspect of the Leviathan encourages us to reconsider the motive behind God's second speech. What is so particularly odd about the way the Leviathan appears here is the fact that God *celebrates* its indomitable features. Although this figure does nothing in Scripture but spar with God, God doesn't deride the Leviathan as a malign opponent. On the contrary, he holds up the Leviathan as a *model* for Job. As the text marvels over this creature, praising it feature by feature, God illustrates what he wants Job to do as well: *fight*. God had received Job's praise. He had absorbed Job's laments. What he would not accept was Job's silence. *Better to act proudly like a king and fight like Leviathan than to remain silent.*

It is the recognition of this motive behind the second divine speech that helps us make sense of the concluding verses of the poetic section of the book (42:1–6). While most of the major English translations of Job render verse 6 as "Therefore, I despise myself, and repent in dust and ashes," it is difficult to square Job's repentance with the rest of the book.[9] Wouldn't Job's repentance signal God's loss of his wager with the Satan? And how could

Job's repentance be followed by God's declaration in verse 7 that Job had spoken *rightly* concerning him whereas Eliphaz and his friends had not?

The solution to this dilemma lies in recognizing that one word in the standard translation of this verse is missing entirely and another has been misunderstood. First, the word *myself* doesn't appear in the Hebrew text at all. Job may have despised or rejected something, but he didn't despise or reject *himself*.[10] Second, the Hebrew expression *wənihamtî 'al* doesn't mean "repent in" but "repent concerning." When we take these two observations together, we can better understand the verse as saying: "Therefore, I reject and repent concerning dust and ashes." Job isn't repenting of sin but of "dust and ashes." But what exactly would this mean?[11]

Samuel Balentine helpfully observes that "dust and ashes" here is a metaphor for silence.[12] It hearkens back to the days when Job sat silently on the ash heap (2:8–13) and to the moment after the first divine speech when Job determined not to speak again:

> I cover my mouth with my hand.
> I spoke once, but I will not answer again,
> > twice, but I will not continue.
>
> > > (40:4–5)

It may even connect with Abraham's repeated reference to himself as "but dush and ashes" as recognition of the fact that he perhaps should have kept silent but instead kept arguing with God over the fate of Sodom and Gomorrah (Gen 18:23–33). When Job rejects and repents of his dust and ashes, he is agreeing with the message of the second divine speech. God didn't want Job's silence. He wanted him to keep lamenting. Job therefore does exactly that: He agrees to turn from his silence and keep lamenting. We see confirmation of this in another line just a few verses earlier. Previously in the divine speeches, it was God who said to Job, "Gird up your loins like a man; I will question you, and you inform me" (38:3; 40:7). Now it is Job who says this to God: "Hear, and I will speak; I will question you, and you inform me" (42:4).

The prose prologue in chapters 1–2 offers one path for grappling with suffering. In these chapters, Job absorbs the blows of his suffering with stoic resolve and remains steadfast in his praise of God. The poetic dialogues found in chapters 3–42 offer an alternative path for times when our ability to praise has been exhausted. In these chapters, Job powerfully laments his continued suffering, and God is willing to receive even the harshest words

Job unleashes. The only response God seems unwilling to tolerate is silence. Offering up words of lament rather than retreating into cold quiet is one of the unique geniuses of our spiritual ancestors. As both the narrative portions of Scripture and the Psalter attest, our ancestors resolved to lament to God in their suffering rather than pretend their suffering did not exist.

Remember That Jesus Also Suffered

Few things play with our minds the way that suffering does. Like water that finds the path of least resistance, suffering floods over us and works its way into the places where we're weakest. It erodes away any superficiality in our beliefs and leaves us vulnerable to doubts and questions we'd rather avoid altogether.

A number of years ago, a young girl mustered the courage to ask Pope Benedict why we suffer. There was a refreshing candor in the pontiff's response:

> I also have the same questions: Why is it this way? Why do you have to suffer so much while others live in ease? And we do not have the answers. But we know that Jesus suffered as you do, an innocent, and that the true God who is revealed in Jesus is by your side.[13]

There is little reason to imagine we will ever fully understand, at least on this side of the veil, why God allows such great suffering. We can, however, take comfort in knowing God also experiences that same suffering in the person of Jesus. We may not understand why God acts as he does, but we can hold on in hope, knowing his actions are born out of shared sympathy with our plight.

10

Seeking God in Death

Who is so strong as to live and never see death?
Who can deliver his own soul from Sheol?
     (Ps 89:48)

Mortality

THE ONLY PARTICULAR "DATE" THAT STANDS OUT in my childhood is 1976. I was a lowly second grader that year, so I was too young to know anything about politics or the economy. The movies I've seen from the period paint a pretty bleak picture of what life must have been like back then. Honestly, how long did it take cities to accumulate that much trash and graffiti? The clothing styles I've seen in those same movies and, I confess, our own family photos suggest a cabal of fashion designers must have played a long and merciless practical joke on society. Surely barbers and hairstylists were in on the gag as well. Again, I was in grammar school, so I don't really remember any of that sort of thing personally. What I do remember is that 1976 was the year of the Bicentennial.

The months leading up to the Fourth of July that year were filled with all sorts of patriotic events. There were cookouts and parades, and every streetlight seemed to have a bit of Americana on it. I had inherited the hobby of coin collecting from my grandfather, so I especially loved those cool new Bicentennial quarters. The best part of that year, though, was the fireworks. I don't know how many fireworks displays I had seen prior to '76, but the show on that Independence Day dwarfed anything I'd ever seen before. In fact, I was so impressed, that I recall turning to my father and asking him to explain again just what exactly a "bicentennial" was. He dutifully explained that it was the two-hundredth anniversary of America's founding. As the gears began to turn in my young brain, I remember replying, "So, that means we'll have to wait another hundred years for the next time they do all this?" My dad affirmed that that was indeed the case. Then, it dawned on me: "But wait, if we have to wait another hundred years, you won't be alive then, will you?" My dad said, "Well, that's true." And that's when it hit me: "If we have to wait another hundred years," I said, "then *I* probably won't be alive then either." I'm sure my dad mumbled something non-committal about this or that, but it didn't matter. This new revelation struck me like a thunderbolt: On the evening of July 4, 1976, at the tender young age of seven, I realized that one day, I was going to die.

Not to be overly dramatic, but there is something disconcerting—if that's the right word—about the fact that one day the world will go on without our being a part of it. My favorite Tolkien poem by far is the one Bilbo offers as he and Frodo sit together in Rivendell on the evening before Frodo and his companions set off to destroy the One Ring. As Bilbo reflects on pleasant memories from summers and autumns past, he arrives at this stanza:

> I sit beside the fire and think
> of how the world will be
> when winter comes without a spring
> that I shall ever see.

A short while later, he muses:

> I sit beside the fire and think
> of people long ago
> and people who will see a world
> that I shall never know.[1]

As human beings, we find ourselves in an unbroken chain of mortality, a line of souls stretching back to Adam who have lived, died, and, in almost every case, ultimately been forgotten. It is not a pleasant thought.

Qoheleth

No book of the Bible wrestles with mortality as intensely as Qoheleth, the book whose title has been cruelly Hellenized and then Latinized to make its way into our Bibles as the inscrutable "Ecclesiastes." The book begins with the line, "The words of Qoheleth, son of David, king in Jerusalem" (Qoh 1:1). "Qoheleth" here is not a name but a title, derived from the Hebrew verb *qāhal*, meaning "to gather." It refers, apparently, to one who "gathers together" *things* (perhaps as a collector of wisdom) or *people* (to address them as a teacher or preacher). The book is often connected with Solomon, though Solomon's name never actually appears in the work. The language of the book, in any case, suggests a time of composition long after the wise king had already passed from the scene. My own view is that the book was composed at a relatively late date but with Solomon in mind as the Teacher or Preacher through whose voice the later sage could express his own reflections concerning the meaning of life. This was a literary device that became increasingly popular in the waning years of the first millennium BC in works such as the Testament of Abraham, the Testament of Job, the books of Enoch, and so forth.

Vanity of Vanities

The first words of Qoheleth give us a sense of the direction the rest of the work will take: "Vanity of vanities! Vanity of vanities! All is vanity!" (1:2). The Hebrew word *hebel*, which I translate here as "vanity," is the key term for the book of Qoheleth as a whole. More than half of the uses of the term in the Hebrew Bible—thirty-eight of seventy-three—are found in just this one short book. Etymologically, *hebel* is connected with notions of "breath" and "vapor," and it is this transitory and insubstantial sense that marks many of the Bible's uses of the term. Job, for example, prays to God: "Leave me alone, for my days are a *breath*" (7:16). Psalm 39 echoes this notion as the psalmist laments:

> Behold, you set my days as a few handbreadths,
>   my lifespan is as nothing before you.
> Each mortal endures only a mere *breath*.
>
> (Ps 39:5)

The insubstantial nature of breath also led biblical authors to use *hebel* in another sense—namely, to capture a sense of "folly," "meaninglessness," and, as I've translated the term here, "vanity." This is not the sort of vanity we associate with prideful obsession about one's appearance but vanity as *without purpose, for nothing*. Psalm 39 also captures this second meaning of *hebel*:

> Surely each person walks about in shadow;
> > surely they make a commotion *for nothing*.[2]
> > > (v. 6)

Job, too, uses the term in this way. He asks, "Why should I grow weary *for nothing*?" (9:29) and demands of his comforters, "Why do you comfort me *with nothing*?" (21:34). Later in the same book, Elihu charges: "Job opens his mouth *with nothing*" (35:16).

At the heart of Qoheleth's contention that "all is vanity" is his inability to see what point there is to life if, at the end of it, we die. Nature itself seems utterly indifferent to its human inhabitants:

> A generation comes, and a generation goes,
> > but the earth stands forever.
>
> The sun rises and the sun sets,
> > and hurries to the place where it rises.
>
> Going to the south and turning round to the north,
> > turning round, turning round, goes the wind,
> > and on its rounds the wind returns.
>
> All the streams run to the sea, but the sea is never full;
> > to the place that the streams run, they return to run again.
> > > (1:4–7)

The cycle of nature continues on relentlessly, but all human efforts within this cycle seem ultimately to amount to nothing. In Qoheleth's words:

> What profit do people gain from the toil
> > that they toil under the sun?
> > > (1:3)

> What has happened will happen;
> > what has been done will be done;
> > there is nothing new under the sun.
> > > (1:9)

It is not as if the figure portrayed in the book had failed to make a search for meaning in the midst of nature's indifferent cycles. On the contrary, Qoheleth applied himself to acquire great wisdom but found no solace there. "In much wisdom is much vexation," he reflects, "and the one who increases knowledge increases pain" (1:17–18). Failing to find meaning in wisdom, he sated himself with every pleasure, but this, too, brought no satisfaction (2:1–11). Ultimately, every human effort and endeavor comes to naught because every human life comes to an end. And what comes after? Nothing that might give meaning to what has come before:

> There is no remembrance of those from earlier times,
>   nor will there be for those who come later.
> There will be no remembrance of them
>   by those who will come after them.
>
>   (1:11)

People are not remembered when they are gone, and the same fate that awaits the fool also awaits the wise (2:16). The spoils we acquire in life pass on to another generation at our death, and who knows what they will do with them (2:18–19; 6:1–2). Qoheleth would surely sympathize with Roy Batty's bitter words in *Blade Runner* over the memories soon to disappear at his death: "All those moments will be lost in time, like tears in the rain."[3]

Life with No Afterlife

Accustomed as we often are to reading the Bible through the lens of its latest literary layers, we can sometimes forget that significant theological developments took place over the course of the biblical period. Some of these are so obvious that we are apt to miss the fact that they are developments at all. There was a time when sacrifices of various sorts were required for all manner of holidays and life events. They started with the voluntary offerings made by Cain and Abel (Gen 4), continued through the spontaneous offerings of the patriarchs (e.g., Gen 12:7; 13:4; 26:25; 33:20), and reached a high level of precision in Israel's priestly literature (cf. Lev 1–16). By the end of the first century AD, however, these sacrifices had ceased. In part because of the destruction of the temple in the year 70, and in part (for Christianity at least) because of the understanding of Jesus' death as the culmination of the sacrificial system, the way we worshiped God changed. This change was dramatic, but truthfully, we largely take it for granted today.

We can observe a more subtle sort of change in an area like Israel's beliefs about monotheism. In the nation's earliest traditions, it seems clear that Israelites—even "orthodox" Israelites—acknowledged the existence of multiple gods. In Exodus 15:11, the Israelites sing, "Who is like you, O Lord, among the gods?" The psalmists praise God as "a great king over all gods" (Ps 95:3) and "the God of gods" (Ps 136:2; cf. Deut 10:17). The description of the Leviathan in Job 41:25 notes that "the gods were afraid at his rising up."[4] The so-called Song of Moses in Deuteronomy 32 mentions the Most High's fixing the boundaries of the nations "according to the number of the gods" (v. 8) and later commands, "Worship him, all you gods!" (v. 43).[5]

Of course, this notion that God was merely *superior* to the other gods would in time prove insufficient. When Elijah laid down his challenge to the people who had been worshiping Baal, he insisted, "If YHWH is God, follow him; if Baal, follow him" (1 Kgs 18:21). Inherent in Elijah's formulation is this key insight: *There can be only one God.* Elijah didn't order the people to follow the strongest of the two deities; he insisted there could only be one and that *one* must be followed.[6] Eventually, Israelite monotheism would reach its peak in the Lord's statements in the second half of Isaiah: "I am YHWH, and there is no other; beside me, there is no God" (Isa 45:5; cf. vv. 6, 18, 21, 22). Stepping back, though, we can see how God met the people of Israel in one place and carried them along to another. There is no scandal in seeing the progress of this theological journey across the pages of Scripture.

What is true of matters like sacrifice and monotheism is also true for Israel's conception of the afterlife. For most of the Old Testament period, there is scant evidence that the Israelites believed death would be followed by either enjoyment of or banishment from the presence of God. The last chapter of the latest book of the Hebrew Bible, Daniel, envisions the resurrection of the dead ("those who sleep") either to everlasting life or everlasting "shame" and "abhorrence" (cf. Dan 12:2). For most of the Old Testament, however, death was thought to be followed by a state best described as "sleep." The persistent refrain for the death of Israel's kings was that they "lay down with their fathers" (cf. 1 Kgs 2:10 [David]; 11:43 [Solomon]; 14:20 [Jeroboam]; 14:31 [Rehoboam]; and so forth). In Psalm 13:3, the psalmist urges God to intervene lest he "sleep the sleep of death." The prophet Jeremiah describes punishment that resembles drunkards drinking until they fall asleep, but in this case, they will "sleep an eternal sleep and never wake" (51:39, 57).

Perhaps the most vivid description of death as sleep is the one Job offers as he sits mourning on the ash heap in Job 3. Given the seemingly unending suffering he is forced to endure, Job wishes he had never been born, and he pronounces maledictions on the day of his birth and night of his conception. In verse 10, he offers as the reason for his curses simply this:

> Because they did not shut the doors of my womb;[7]
>   and hid trouble from my eyes.

He then goes on to ask in verses 11–12:

> Why did I not die from the womb,
>   come forth from the belly and perish?
> Why were there knees to receive me,
>   why breasts that I should nurse?

If this life of suffering is all that God intended for him, Job wants to know why God let him be conceived at all. Why couldn't he have simply died in the womb? Why couldn't he have been discarded to die as an infant? Death would be preferable to the suffering he now has to endure:

> For now, I would be lying down, I would be quiet;
>   I would be asleep then; I would be at rest.
>   (v. 13)

This notion of death as sleep is not reserved for righteous Job alone; all people, regardless of status or character, go to the same fate. "I would be at rest," Job insists,

> with kings and counselors of the earth,
>   those who build ruins[8] for themselves,
> or with princes possessing gold,
>   who fill their houses with silver.
> Why was I not buried like a stillborn child,
>   like infants who do not see the light?
> There the wicked cease their troubling,
>   and there rest those who have exhausted their strength.
> The captives are at ease together;
>   they no longer hear the voice of their taskmaster.
> Both the small and the great are there,
>   and the slave is free of his masters.
>   (13b–19)

Elsewhere, Job's description of what awaits us after death strikes a more negative tone. In these passages, he speaks less of the welcome rest death provides and instead highlights death's permanency. Responding to one miserable comforter, he insists:

> The eye that gazes upon me will see me no more;
> > your eyes may bend toward me, but I will not be there.
> The cloud fades and goes away;
> > so the one who goes down to Sheol does not come up.
> He returns no more to his home;
> > he is no longer acknowledged in his place.
> > > (7:8–10)

Later, he adds:

> Are not my days but a few? Cease!
> > Leave me alone that I might be cheerful for a moment,
> before I go—and I shall not return—
> > to the land of darkness and deadly shadow,
> a land of gloom like thick darkness,
> > a land of deadly shadow without order,
> > where light is like thick darkness.
> > > (10:20–22)

Job's reflections on his seemingly imminent death are echoed in the Psalter. The mournful strains of Psalm 88 are so desperate, in part, because the psalmist considers death to be a place of no return:

> Do you work wonders for the dead?
> > Will the shades rise up and praise you?
> Is your steadfast love recounted in the grave,
> > your faithfulness in Abaddon?[9]
> Are your wonders made known in darkness,
> > your righteousness in the land that is forgotten?
> > > (vv. 10–12)

Note that each of these questions is rhetorical; each expects a *negative* answer. The psalmist does *not* believe the dead rise up and praise God, nor does he believe God's actions extend to those beyond the grave. If God lets the psalmist die, then the chance for the psalmist to praise God will be at an end.

Qoheleth's Crisis

Qoheleth's grappling with mortality isn't born of the same sort of intense suffering experienced by Job or the psalmist. His more reflective musings veer instead toward the philosophical. It's not that Qoheleth has ceased to believe in God; on the contrary, the very fact that he *does* believe in God has led him to his present intellectual crisis. It is God who "has set eternity in humanity's heart," but we humans remain unable "to discern the work God has done from beginning to end" (3:11). The blade that suddenly cuts the cord of our existence at death leaves us unable to know whether our accomplishments in this life have any genuine meaning. Qoheleth goes so far as to question whether the fate of humans is ultimately any different than that of beasts:

> I decided in my heart, as it concerns human beings, to distinguish them from God and to show that they themselves are beasts. For the fate of human beings and the fate of beasts is the same fate; as one dies, so the other dies; both share one spirit. The human has no advantage over the beast, because all is vanity. Both go to one place; both are from the dust, and both return to the dust. Who knows whether the spirit of human beings goes upward and the spirit of the beast goes down into the earth?
> (3:18–21)

With words of this sort, it is fair to say we are witnessing the last gasps of a theology that lacks any hope for an afterlife. Though Qoheleth himself would not be the one to strike a new path out of this seeming dead end, other writers in Israel soon would.

Belief in a Just God

Death is never pleasant, but at the end of a long and happy life, when the infirmities of old age have begun to accumulate, there is a sense in which death can be a kind of release. In these circumstances, we might hear an echo of elderly Simeon who had waited a lifetime to see Israel's promised Messiah. As he held the Christ-child in his arms, he said with relief, "Master, now you release your servant in peace according to your word" (Luke 2:29). In the early years of Israel's history, years when the nation was growing from one lone couple to a mighty nation, years marked by deliverance and conquest and expansion, it was perhaps understandable that the people could look at the days of *this life* as satisfying enough. When lives are long and there is relative peace and prosperity, God's promises of blessing and protection ring true. But what of the nation's condition after the fateful eighth century BC, when a long line of empires began to rob Israel and Judah of any semblance of peace? First came the Assyrians who conquered the north in 722. A century later, it would be the Babylonians who conquered the south in 605. These would be followed by the Persians in 539, the Greeks in 332, the Egyptian Ptolemies in 301, the Syrian Seleucids in 198, and the Romans in 63. Here and there would be brief bright spots—a few years of peace under Hezekiah and Josiah, a momentary window of independence after the Maccabean Revolt—but for the most part, the nation was consigned to languish under the heel of one foreign oppressor after another, and it would continue to do so long after the writing of Scripture had come to an end.

During these long centuries of oppression, the nation might have been tempted to reevaluate its view of God, to concede that the gods of the nations were more powerful than their God, YHWH. The Assyrian emperor Sennacherib practically begged the Judeans to admit this was the case when he arrayed his forces against Jerusalem:

> Who among all the gods of the nations has been able to save their lands from my hand that YHWH should be able to save Jerusalem from my hand?
>
> (1 Kgs 18:35)

But even as one empire passed control of the land of Israel to another, the faithful steadfastly refused to acknowledge the superiority of the so-called gods of other nations. Quite the contrary, these centuries witnessed a steady *elevation* of the power and status of YHWH in the minds of the biblical authors. The language of the latter part of Isaiah, written at a time of transition from Babylon to Persia, reflects an understanding of God's supremacy essentially unmatched in any ancient literature—Israelite or non-Israelite—written before it (see especially Isa 40, 45). But if the Israelites continued to believe God was powerful, surely over the course of their centuries of suffering they must have concluded he was not, in fact, just. The nation must be suffering because YHWH was a tyrant, unheeding of the people's plight. This, however, wasn't Israel's conclusion either. Instead, the prophets endlessly trumpeted God's righteousness and justice (just in Isaiah, see 41:10; 45:21; 53:11). And it was in the intersection of these two beliefs about

God—belief in his great power and in his perfect justice—that the seeds for a way out of Qoheleth's dilemma were planted.

As the centuries of foreign domination rolled on, the prophets of Israel became increasingly insistent that if God's justice was not evident now, it *would be* evident in the future. "In that day," the prophets insisted again and again, God's justice will be revealed.[10] And if the nation's conviction concerning God's justice was strong enough to hold that the mighty empires that oppressed Israel would be defeated (cf. Isa 10; 47; Jer 25:12), that the scattered exiles would be restored (Isa 27; Jer 23), and that Jerusalem would be rebuilt (Isa 44; 52; 66; Jer 30–31), then that conviction was surely strong enough to believe God's justice would be exercised if not in this world, *then in the world to come*. At its most basic level, belief in the afterlife is a statement of faith concerning the justice of God. It is the sort of conviction that Peter shared with his readers as they faced suffering of their own:

> Though you have not seen him, you love him. And though you do not see him now, you believe in him and rejoice with joy inexpressible and glorious, obtaining as the outcome of your faith, the salvation of your souls.
>
> (1 Pet 1:8–9)

With our belief in the afterlife, we make our ultimate statement concerning who we believe God to be. As we hold out hope for the salvation of our souls, we refuse to let the injustice of our present circumstances overwhelm our belief in God's justice and power.

Seeking God in Death

In the end, death comes to us all. For some of us, death will come suddenly and unexpectedly, leaving us with little opportunity to consider the deeper significance of either life or death. For others of us, death will come more slowly and more predictably. For those who live to see death's steady approach, how can we seek God as it arrives?

Remember Your Creator

There are echoes of Qoheleth's somber reflections in Matthew Arnold's famous poem "Dover Beach." Like Qoheleth, Arnold is deeply affected by the seemingly endless cycle of the natural world, in his case exemplified by the ebb and flow of the sea:

> Listen! you hear the grating roar
> Of pebbles which the waves draw back, and fling,
> At their return, up the high strand,
> Begin, and cease, and then again begin,
> With tremulous cadence slow, and bring
> The eternal note of sadness in.

More in sorrow than in anger, he observes that "the Sea of Faith," once at high tide like the sea he witnessed at Dover Beach, now recedes, leaving only

> Its melancholy, long, withdrawing roar,
> Retreating, to the breath
> Of the night-wind, down the vast edges drear
> And naked shingles of the world.

Absent faith, Arnold's assessment of the world is at once honest and bleak. The world which seems

> To lie before us like a land of dreams,
> So various, so beautiful, so new,
> Hath really neither joy, nor love, nor light,
> Nor certitude, nor peace, nor help for pain;
> And we are here as on a darkling plain
> Swept with confused alarms of struggle and flight,
> Where ignorant armies clash by night.

Arnold sounds only one positive note in his elegy for faith. To the one whom he has bidden, "Come to the window, sweet is the night-air," he urges, "Ah, love, let us be true to one another!" Lacking hope, Arnold seeks to find what comfort he can in the loving companionship of another person.

Qoheleth would doubtless resonate with Arnold's pessimistic assessment of the state of the world, and he would surely have no qualms with Arnold's desire to find solace in the love of another (cf. Qoh 9:9). Qoheleth was unwilling, though, to follow the path Arnold took in leaving faith behind. However great his struggles with human mortality, Qoheleth pursued and encouraged others to pursue his God. The closing chapter of the book begins with the memorable words, "Remember your Creator" (12:1). Doubtless as a reflection of his nagging thoughts on death, however, Qoheleth carries this sentiment one step further, saying not only "Remember your Creator" but "Remember your Creator *in the days of your youth*, before evil days come, and years reach you of which you will say, 'I have no pleasure in them.'"

It is a commonplace, at least in Western society, for young people to imagine they should sow their wild oats in youth and then settle down later to a more respectable life of career and family and, perhaps, even God. Qoheleth turns this paradigm upside down. Our later years—if later years we are granted—are weighed down by the many cares of life, cares that hold us back from serving God as we might. To this, we can add the breakdown of our youthful bodies that inevitably comes. Qoheleth describes the frailties of old age in richly symbolic language. Our vision dims—"sun and moon and stars grow dark, and the clouds return after the rain" (v. 2). Our hands shake—"the keepers of the house tremble" (v. 3a). Our stature becomes stooped—"the men of valor are bent" (v. 3b). Our teeth are often lost—"the maids that grind cease working because they are too few" (v. 3c). Our hearing declines—"the sound of the mill grows low . . . and all the daughters of song are muffled" (v. 4). We wake with the dawn—"One rises at the song of a bird" (v. 4). We grow fearful of the unknown—"One is fearful of the heights, and terror is on the road" (v. 5a). Our hair turns white—"the almond tree blossoms" (v. 5b). Sexual desire wanes—"the grasshopper drags itself along, and desire fails" (v. 5c). And then, finally, our life comes to an end:

> The silver cord is snapped, and the golden bowl is broken. The pitcher is broken at the spring, and the wheel is smashed at the cistern. The dust returns to the earth as it was before, and the spirit returns to the God who gave it.
>
> (vv. 6–7)

If we would seek an elusive God, there is no time like the present to do so. Better to pursue God while we are young, to chase after him while we are still in the prime of life, than to wait until that pursuit is burdened down with a lifetime of cares and sorrows.

A life spent from its youth in pursuit of God offers another benefit beyond merely youthful energy to serve. It is this kind of life that it avoids many of the wounds we inflict on our hearts when we spend years *not* pursuing God. Psalm 1 begins with the words, "O the happinesses of the person who . . . ," but then immediately proceeds to list what the happy person *does not do.* The happy person "*does not walk* in the counsel of the wicked, and in the way of sinners *does not stand*, and in the seat of scoffers *does not sit.*" The repeated "no, no, no" of these lines, more evident in Hebrew even than in English, seems counterintuitive. Who defines happiness by the word *no*? But there's a hidden genius in the psalmist's lines. Consider how much happiness we gain by saying no to those things that harm us. The bad things we do leave scars on our hearts that never truly go away. The psalmist would steer us away from these hurts. Qoheleth would steer us away from them from our earliest days of youth.

Number Our Days

The beautiful Psalm 90—truthfully, my favorite psalm—strikes a marked contrast between God's time and our time. The psalmist begins with the memorable line:

> O Lord, you have been a refuge for us,
> > from generation to generation.
> > > (v. 1)

"Refuge" seems to suggest a geographical locale, perhaps suggesting God has provided a safe *space* for us to live. The verse that follows, however, makes clear that it is within God's *time* that we exist:

> Before the mountains were born
> > or you had given birth to the earth and the world,
> > from eternity to eternity, you are God.
> > > (v. 2)

God's time is infinite; it stretches "from eternity to eternity." By contrast, our time is so very finite. Verse 3 reflects:

> You turn frail humans back to dust,
> > saying, "Return, O mortals!"

From dust we came and to dust we will return, and all at just a word from God; this is our time. Verse 4, however, returns to God's time:

> For a thousand years in your eyes
> > are like yesterday when it has passed,
> > or like a watch in the night.

Note that the psalmist doesn't use the familiar expression "a thousand years are like one day." Instead, he compares a thousand years in God's sight to "yesterday" and to "a watch in the night." A moment's reflection reminds us that *yesterday* is no longer a full day at all. Though it may have taken twenty-four hours for us to experience that day when it was still *today*, once past, it begins to recede in our minds until only bits and pieces are left to us. The same is true with a watch *in the night*. This is a watch that passes *while we are asleep*, gone seemingly in a moment's time without our even being aware of its passing.

Verses 5–6 return to our time:

You sweep them away; they are like a dream.[11]
    They are like grass that grows anew in the morning.
In the morning, it sprouts and grows anew;
    by evening, it wilts and withers.

There is no "eternity to eternity" in our time. The psalmist suggests we are more like tender grass that sprouts in the morning and withers by evening. In one of the more sobering lines in Scripture, he offers in verse 9:

All our days pass away under your wrath;
    we bring our years to an end with a sigh.

Given the immense gap between God's time and our time, we might reasonably conclude that the answer to our mortal dilemma would be to gain more time. The psalmist, however, finds this solution to be lacking:

The span of our life is seventy years,
    or perhaps eighty years if we are strong.
But the greater part of them is but toil and sorrow,
    for they pass by quickly, and we fly away.
                   (v. 10)

The psalmist recognizes that having an additional decade of life is a mixed blessing. Sadly, living to age eighty doesn't mean gaining an extra decade of "twenties"; instead, we add a decade of "seventies." Longer life means only more toil and more sorrow, and even these difficult years soon pass us by.

But if more time is not the psalmist's prescription, what is? Here, we find the key line of the psalm. Faced with a God whose time vastly outstrips our own, faced with difficult years that are all too brief, the psalmist asks God in verse 12:

> Teach us to number our days rightly,
>   so we may gain a heart of wisdom.

He makes no plea about gaining more days of life; he asks instead that we be able to make the best use of the days we have. He asks God to teach us to number our days, to treat them as the precious commodity they are, to treasure each one.

Because it plays such a prominent role in the movie *Dead Poet's Society*, the phrase *carpe diem*, "seize the day," may seem overly trite. If we can look past the—God forbid—popularity of the phrase, however, there is a keen insight in the sentiment it conveys. Early in the movie, John Keating (the lead character, played by Robin Williams) quotes a line from a poem by Robert Herrick:

> Gather ye rosebuds while ye may,
> Old time is still a-flying;
> And this same flower that smiles today
> Tomorrow will be dying.[12]

These are sentiments similar to those expressed by A. E. Housman as he reflects on cherry trees in bloom, "wearing white for Eastertide." Echoing Psalm 90, he says:

> Now, of my threescore years and ten,
> Twenty will not come again,
> And take from seventy springs a score,
> It only leaves me fifty more.
> And since to look at things in bloom
> Fifty springs are little room,
> About the woodlands I will go
> To see the cherry hung with snow.[13]

The distance between Herrick's "Gather ye rosebuds while ye may," Keating's "*carpe diem*," Housman's "fifty springs are little room," and Psalm 90's "Teach us to number our days" is vanishingly small. Death waits—sometimes patiently, sometimes impatiently—for each one of us. We seek God best when we treasure each day he has allotted to us.

Leave a Good Name

Psalm 90 draws to a close in verse 17 with a twice-repeated prayer:

> Establish the work of our hands!
> Establish the work of our hands!

The verb the psalmist repeats in these lines—the verb I translate here as "establish"—is often connected with the establishment or founding of a structure, an institution, or even the fundamental parts of creation. God *establishes* his sanctuary (Exod 15:17), his throne (Ps 9:7), the throne of his anointed king (2 Sam 7:13), Jerusalem (Ps 48:8; Isa 62:7), and the moon, stars, and heavens (Ps 8:3; Prov 3:19). At the heart of the term is its sense of permanency, solidity, and endurance. This constitutes the great hope of the psalmist. Having come to grips with the fact that the span of his life is limited, the psalmist asks God to teach him to number his days, to treat his days like the precious commodity they are. And then, having done so, he asks God to crown what he has accomplished with a divinely graced longevity. He hopes to see the works of his hands remain and prosper after his own days come to an end.

When we seek God with the knowledge that death looms before us, whether far away or uncomfortably close, it should spur us to create legacies that will live on and continue to honor God even when we're gone. Perhaps the most important legacy we have to offer, and the one most within our control, is that of *a good name*. In Proverbs 10:7, the sage insists:

> The memory of the righteous is a blessing,
> but the name of the wicked will rot.

Precious few of us will achieve fame so great that our name and reputation will be remembered in centuries to come. But with care, our name can be remembered fondly by our children and even our children's children. In the closing lines of *A Tale of Two Cities*, as Sydney Carton is brought before the guillotine, he looks forward with hope to a time when a son would be born who would bear his name. That son would not be his own but would instead be born to the couple Carton was giving his life to rescue and reunite. He sees in that child who will bear his name "a man winning his way up in that path of life which once was mine. I see him winning it so well, that my name is made illustrious there by the light of his. I see the blots I threw upon it, faded away."[14] With one great final act, Carton could hope to clear his name of years of rakish dissipation.

Most of us will not be so fortunate to see the coffers of our reputation suddenly refilled in death if we have so thoroughly emptied them in life. Leaving the legacy of a good name is rather a matter of slow deposits made year after year, carefully saved and not squandered on actions that bring shame to it. If we love our children, care for them as we are able, model before them a sober and righteous life, and work to pass along to them the candle of faith we ourselves have tended, then we will hold a special place in their hearts that will help them seek God as well. And what is true of our own children will be true of others who come into our care. Sons- and daughters-in-law, nieces and nephews, friends we come to think of as relatives—all of these can share in the treasury of faith we leave behind.

11

Seeking God in Joy

Let the ransomed of the LORD *return,*
   and come to Zion with shouts of rejoicing,
   and with everlasting joy upon their heads.
Gladness and joy let them find;
   and may sorrow and sighing flee away!
      (Isa 51:11)

Unhappy Endings

WHEN THE PROPHET JEHU CAME CALLING to execute a death sentence on wicked Jezebel, the infamous queen seemed determined to go out in style. The author of 2 Kings tells us that when Jezebel heard the prophet was coming, "She painted her eyes and adorned her head and went to look out the window" (9:30). Beautiful though she may have been at that moment, her fate would be a gruesome one. At the prophet's summons, some of the queen's own servants threw her from the window, where horses trampled her body and dogs devoured all but her hands, feet, and skull. Jezebel's was a bitter ending, masked by a beautiful facade.

A great many things could fit the description of beautiful but bitter. The Pietà by Michelangelo that graces one of the chapels of St. Peter's Basilica is a work of almost indescribable beauty, but its subject matter—the mother of

Jesus holding her lifeless son—is every bit as bitter as the sculpture is beautiful. Peter Paul Rubens' depiction of Samson and Delilah shares a similar quality. Rubens captures the scene with characteristic lavishness. The lighting is delicately soft, the carpets plush, and the folds of silken fabrics shimmer with rich, bold hues of purple and red and gold. As Samson sleeps at Delilah's breast, one could almost take him for a son resting on his mother's lap. But then we see the wizened old woman holding a candle for a servant to cut away Samson's locks and at the door the Philistine soldiers who will soon gouge out his eyes and haul him away as a captive. Beautiful and bitter.

Devotees of Shakespeare need not look far to find beautiful but bitter endings in the Bard's plays. We are warned in the very first lines of *Romeo and Juliet* that a tragic end awaits the young couple:

> A pair of star-crossed lovers take their life;
> Whose misadventured piteous overthrows
> Doth with their death bury their parents' strife.
> The fearful passage of their death-marked love
> And the continuance of their parents' rage,
> Which, but their children's end, naught could remove.

But Shakespeare's beautiful language beguiles us into hoping the story's ending will be beautiful as well. When "the two hours' traffic of our stage" comes to an end, we "go hence to have more talk of these sad things," still in disbelief that something so beautiful could end so bitterly. Some readers have found stories like *Romeo and Juliet* too sad to bear and have actually altered the works to give them happy endings. The German composer Georg Benda did so in his 1776 opera *Romeo and Julie*, as did Sergei Prokofiev in a 1935 ballet based on Shakespeare's play. Nahum Tate, one of Britain's poet laureates, rewrote the bitter ending to *King Lear*, restoring the king to his throne, sparing Cordelia, and marrying her off to Edgar.[1] Over the years, Hollywood has performed similar surgery on all manner of stories, from Ernest Hemingway's *A Farewell to Arms* to Victor Hugo's *Hunchback of Notre Dame* to the Brothers Grimm's *Cinderella*.

Some stories are hard. They are bitter indeed, and our hearts hurt to hear them. In a particularly touching scene in *The Lord of the Rings*, Sam and Frodo are struck by the realization that their seemingly hopeless quest to destroy the Ring is actually just the continuation of a story that began many ages before them. Sam wonders if their part in it will be put into words and "told by the fireside, or read out of a great big book with red and black letters, years and years afterwards." They smile at the thought of a young hobbit, years hence, wanting to hear about Frodo, "the famousest of the hobbits," and "Samwise the stouthearted." But then Frodo reflects, "You and I, Sam, are still stuck in the worst places of the story and it is all too likely that some will say at this point: 'Shut the book now, dad; we don't want to read any more.'"[2]

We have traveled through some deep waters in this book, and particularly in the last few chapters. Doubt, suffering, and death are gloomy subjects, and they aren't made any brighter by God's elusiveness in the midst of them. It would be tempting to simply make an abrupt shift and tack a happy ending onto this volume. Or perhaps we might echo the young hobbit's sentiments and merely shut the book because we don't want to read anymore. I would like, however, to strike out on a different path. Granting that those in pursuit of God will suffer seasons of doubt, granting that all of us will endure times of suffering, granting that our suffering coalesces in the greatest indignity of all, death, there remains still one more area in which we can seek after God: *joy*. Amidst all those varied moments of suffering and doubt, there are also interspersed moments of another sort, moments when we see the face of God in the happiest moments of life.

Qoheleth Redux

In the preceding chapter, we followed the contours of Qoheleth's grim struggle with human mortality. Qoheleth made his contribution to the canon at a time before ancient Israel took for granted the concept of a differentiated afterlife in which some souls went on to enjoy the eternal presence of God and other souls did not. With little hope for existence *after* death, Qoheleth came to lose hope for meaning *before* death. He lamented the fact that we will soon be forgotten after we die (1:11) and that the produce of our life's labors will be left to others who may well squander what we leave behind (2:18–19; 6:1–2). Ultimately, he remained agnostic even as to whether the ultimate fate of human beings is any different than that of beasts (3:19–21). A surplus of optimism was clearly not one of Qoheleth's problems.

Qoheleth is a difficult book. To return to the language used above, it is a bitter book or at least a book that dares to look squarely at a bitter problem. There is also a certain beauty to it, though. Nearly everyone is familiar— some through the Bible and some through The Byrds—with at least one of the book's poems:

> There is a season for everything,
>   and a time for every matter under the heavens.
> A time to give birth, and a time to die.
> A time to plant, and a time to uproot what is planted.
> A time to kill, and a time to heal.
> A time to tear down, and a time to rebuild.
> A time to weep, and a time to rejoice.
> A time to mourn, and a time to dance.
> A time to cast stones, and a time to gather stones.
> A time to embrace, and a time to refrain from embracing.
> A time to seek, and a time to give up as lost.
> A time to keep, and a time to cast away.
> A time to tear apart, and a time to sew together.
> A time to be silent, and a time to speak.
> A time to love, and a time to hate.
> A time of war, and a time of peace.
>
> (3:1–8)

It is a beautiful poem, and there is beauty to be found in Qoheleth's language elsewhere. There is also something beautiful in the message Qoheleth conveys to those who share his intellectual struggle. Though we may find it impossible to fully grasp God's plan (3:11; 8:16–17; 11:5), though we often see injustice where there should be justice, wickedness where there should be righteousness (3:16), though it may be "an unfortunate business that God has given humans to be concerned with" (1:13), Qoheleth still has a word of instruction for us. He urges us to live, to find joy while we can, to lay hold of what is good in life while we're able.

Consider these passages that stand alongside Qoheleth's words of despair and often form the conclusions to his major sections:

> There is nothing better for a person than to eat and drink and let themselves enjoy what is good amidst all their toil. This, too, I saw was from the hand of God.
>
> (2:24–25)

> I know that there is nothing better for them than that they rejoice and do what is good during their lives. Indeed, it is the gift of God that a person should eat and drink and enjoy what is good in the midst of all their toil.
>
> (3:13)

> Behold, what I have seen to be good and beautiful is to eat and to drink and to enjoy what is good amidst all the toil that one toils under the sun during the few days of life that God gives a person as their lot.
> (5:18)

> There is nothing better for a person under the sun than to eat and to drink and to rejoice. This, at least, will accompany them in their toil, in the days of life that God has given them under the sun.
> (8:15)

"To eat and to drink and to enjoy what is good" is a thematic catchphrase in Qoheleth every bit as important as his more famous "Vanity of vanities, all is vanity!" It may be our lot to suffer, but it is also our lot to receive certain blessings and pleasures from God. We should embrace the latter even as we endure the former.

Seeking God in Joy

Qoheleth's struggle to find meaning in the world is, at its base, a struggle with God's elusiveness. God's justice can be hard to perceive when "the righteous perish in their righteousness and the wicked prolong their lives through their evil ways" (7:15). God's love can be difficult to fathom when life is hard and its hardship comes to an end only with death. Qoheleth's struggles with God's elusiveness, though, are balanced with promptings to continue our search for God. He urges us to seek God in the moments of joy God has allotted to us. How then can we seek God in joy?

Savor What Is Best in Creation

The approach of historic Judaism and Christianity to life is not libertine, but neither is it ascetic. It neither grants us permission to do as we please nor forbids us to enjoy any pleasure at all. Though often derided as if it were simply a matter of ritual and obligation, Israel's sacrificial system was actually centered around the notion of enjoying a festive meal with God. To be sure, there were sacrifices like burnt offerings and purification offerings that served other purposes, but the most common sacrifice—the fellowship offering—was one in which both God and the person offering the sacrifice received meat, bread, and oil (Lev 7). This festive element carried over to offerings of firstfruits as well. As we saw in chapters 4 (on nature) and 6 (on worship), when the Israelites began their harvest, they were to present a basket of their produce to the priest and rehearse God's mighty acts in the exodus and conquest (Deut 26:5–10). Not to be missed is the instruction that follows the rehearsal of that creedal statement:

> Then you shall *rejoice* over all the goodness that the LORD your God has given to you and to your household, you and the Levite and the sojourner in your midst.
> (v. 11)

The offering of firstfruits was to be followed by a celebration. Deuteronomy 14 gives similar instructions concerning the tithes the Israelites were to bring to the house of God. Because God's blessing could be so great that it would be a burden to transport the tithe to the shrine, the law encouraged the people to convert their produce to money ("silver") and take that money to God's appointed place. There, they are told:

> You may spend the money for whatever your heart [lit. "throat"] desires: cattle, sheep, wine, strong drink, or whatever your heart ["throat"] should ask for. You shall eat it there, both you and your household, before the LORD your God.
> (v. 26)

There is certainly no hint of asceticism in these verses.

Given this background of worship as festive celebration, it is little wonder that Israel's prophets looked to God's restoration of the nation and his ingathering of its exiles as a time of feasting. Isaiah proclaims:

> On this mountain, the LORD of hosts will prepare for all peoples
>   a succulent feast, a feast of reserved wines,
>   rich meats with marrow, reserved wines well refined.
> (25:6)

Even Jeremiah, whose prophecies are so often filled with foreboding and despair, foresees:

> They shall come and sing for joy on the heights of Zion;
>   they shall be radiant over the goodness of the LORD,
> over the grain and the new wine and the oil,
>   over the young of the sheep and cattle.

> Their throats shall be like a watered garden,
>> and they shall languish no more.
> Then the virgin will rejoice in the dance,
>> and the young men and old together as well.
> I will turn their mourning to joy;
>> I will comfort them and give them joy in place of their grief.
> I will sate the throats of the priests with fatness,
>> and my people will be satisfied with my goodness.
>
> (31:12–14)

These prophetic expectations for the celebratory restoration of Zion pave the way for similar expressions in the New Testament. The book of Revelation famously describes the "marriage supper of the Lamb" (19:7–9), and Jesus himself anticipates a time when "many will come from east and west and eat with Abraham, Isaac, and Jacob in the kingdom of heaven" (Matt 8:10–11; cf. Luke 13:29). The Messiah offers a foretaste of the heavenly banquet to come in his eating and drinking with those he sought to reach. He feeds the multitudes (Matt 14; 15; Mark 6; 8; Luke 9; John 10), provides wine—apparently the best of wines—at the wedding at Cana in Galilee (John 2:1–11), and eats even with those deemed sinners by the religious authorities of his day (Matt 11:19; Mark 2:16; Luke 5:30; 7:34). In the final hours before the cross, the one thing Jesus confesses he wanted to do was to share a feast with his disciples: "I have eagerly desired to eat this Passover with you before I suffer" (Luke 22:15).

The theme of feasting that wends its way through Scripture is grounded in an idea we previously considered—namely, that our spiritual ancestors reckoned the bounty of creation to be a blessing from God. Psalm 104 insists it is God who "sends forth springs in the wadis" to "give drink to all his creatures in the fields" (vv. 10–11). It is God who "waters the mountains from his upper chambers" so that "the earth is satisfied by the fruit of his works" (v. 13). And it is God who cares for humans as well:

> He causes grass to sprout for the cattle,
>> and plants for humanity's labor,
> to bring forth bread from the earth,
>> and wine to rejoice the human heart,
> to make the face shine with oil,
>> and to strengthen the human heart with bread.
>
> (vv. 14–15)

Note the chiastic structure in the psalmist's description of the blessings God provides. The staple of the Israelites' diet, bread, is mentioned first and last ("to bring forth bread" and "bread to strengthen"), but in between these two rest more extravagant blessings: "wine to rejoice the heart" and "oil to make the face shine." God's creation not only supplies our basic needs but also gives us luxuries as well.

It is the indissoluble tie between creation's delights and God's blessing that opens up a path for us to seek God in joy. It is God who "causes his sun to rise upon the evil and the good and sends rain upon the just and the unjust" (Matt 5:45), and the bounties of harvesttime are gifts from a good God to his needy children.

One of my favorite memories of our time in Boston was our family's trek to Smolak Farms each fall to go apple picking. Like much of the sylvan areas north of Boston, this particular apple orchard looked as if it had been plucked straight from a poem by Robert Frost. The leaves of the surrounding forests were nearly at their peak of autumn orange and yellow. The heady fragrance of apples was everywhere, from the cups of apple cider in our hands to the apples still clinging to branches of the trees. We would move from row to row, lifting our then very young sons up to pick the fruit they deemed the best. And at the end of the day, my wife would always turn part of our harvest into a pie we could savor for days to come. These were almost perfect times. They were moments of rest and play and family and food and drink all woven into one. These were moments of joy to be savored. Tomatoes and peaches in summertime, ripe apples in fall, a fresh-baked loaf of bread, a well-aged wine—all of these are gifts intended to remind us that even on the difficult path we tread in life, God has provided blessings along the way. The same shepherd who leads us through the valley of the shadow of death sets a table before us, anoints our head with oil, and makes our cup overflow.

Fall In Love

It is said of parenting that the days are long but the years are short. Qoheleth would argue that the same is true for life itself. Our days seem long because of the hardships we endure, and yet in the end those same days seem far too few. Recognizing that this is our lot in life, Qoheleth urges us to embrace the rest of what God has allotted to us; he encourages us to eat and to drink and to enjoy what is good in the world God has made. But Qoheleth's counsel in this regard reaches beyond mere food and drink; the Teacher also offers a word concerning love:

> Go, eat your bread with joy, and drink your wine with a happy heart, for God has already accepted your works. At all times, let your clothes be white, and let not oil be lacking from your head. *Enjoy life with a wife you love all the days of this life of vanity that has been allotted to you under the sun.*
>
> (9:7–9a)

Like most biblical literature—and most ancient literature, and most literature of any kind until quite recently—the book of Qoheleth was written to a largely male audience. It's no surprise, then, that the author mentions only enjoying life "with *a wife* you love," and it would do no great violence to the text to say simply, "with *a spouse* you love." Key for us is rather the fact that Qoheleth regards the lifelong companionship of a spouse as another of God's blessings *to be enjoyed*. The author's expression here is literally, "See life," but the Hebrew verb "see" often means "experience" and is regularly used in this fashion in Qoheleth to urge us to "enjoy what is good" (cf. 2:1, 24; 3:13; 5:17; 6:6). Qoheleth's counsel is to "see life," to "enjoy life," with someone we love.

There is doubtless a sexual component to what Qoheleth encourages. Other biblical texts are certainly not shy on this subject. It is hard not to smile at the man's excited reaction to seeing the woman in the account of the first marriage in Eden. Having named the animals and discovered that none corresponded to him, the man sees the naked woman and exclaims, "This one—finally!—is bone of my bones and flesh of my flesh!" (Gen 2:23). The tender description of Jacob's love for Rachel during his seven years of service for her—"they seemed but a few days in his eyes because of his love for her"—is balanced by his forthright demand to Rachel's father when his service was complete: "Give me my wife that I may go in to her" (Gen 29:20–21). The double entendre in this phrase is as strong in Hebrew as it is in English (cf. Gen 16:2; 29:23, 30; 30:3, 4, 16; 38:8; Deut 22:13; 2 Sam 16:21). Perhaps most forceful in this regard is the advice from father to son in Proverbs 5. Warning his son to steer clear of adultery, the father urges:

> Drink water from your own cistern,
>   streams from your own well. . . .
> Let your fountain be blessed,
>   and find joy in the wife of your youth,

> a loving doe, a graceful mountain ewe.
> Let her breasts satisfy you at all times;
> be always intoxicated with her love.
>
> (vv. 15, 18–19)

These lines contain their own share of subtle double entendres. The "cistern," "well," and "fountain" in the passage are not only metaphorical but also hint at female genitalia (see Lev 12:7; 20:18), and the verb translated here as "satisfy" refers primarily to "letting one drink abundantly." The father is straightforward in his encouragement to his son to delight in the physical pleasures of his wife.

There is more, though, than sex in Qoheleth's encouragement to hold tight to a loving spouse. Elsewhere, it is the vital importance of *companionship* that Qoheleth emphasizes. In chapter 4, he links together a series of wise observations underscoring this point:

> Two are better than one, because they have better wages for their toil. For if one falls, a friend can help him up, but woe to the one who falls and does not have another to help him up. Again, if two lie down together, they can keep warm, but how can one person alone warm himself? If one attacks, two can stand up to him, and a threefold cord is not easily snapped.
>
> (vv. 9–12)

What is true for friends is doubly true for a husband and wife. The companionship of a man and woman committed to one another for life is more profitable ("better wages"), more helpful ("help him up"), more comforting ("keep warm"), and more protective ("two can stand up") than any regular friendship. To return once more to Eden, the man and woman were not complete by themselves; they needed the companionship of the other to truly be "good." And if it is true that we see a bit of the divine in other people because each of us bears the image of God, then this should be especially true for the person who loves us most and longest and who sacrifices most on our behalf. Our spouse is not just a companion but a reflection of God in our midst. When we cultivate that loving relationship with our spouse, we create moments of joy for ourselves and steer ourselves back toward the God who authored the very notion of companionship.

There is one other aspect of this dynamic that bears at least brief mention. I would argue that each of the Bible's wisdom books helps us see

God in ways that, perhaps, fall outside of the traditional, covenantal path. Proverbs helps us see God in the orderliness and rationality of the world; the world works because God has made it work. Job helps us see God in times of suffering; even when we don't understand the "why" of life, we can still press on toward the God we hope will deliver us. Qoheleth helps us see God as we consider our own mortality; the reality of death helps us clarify what and who is important. But what of Song of Songs? What are we to do with this odd collection of love poetry tucked between the wisdom books and the prophets? I believe the book is meant to help us see God when we fall in love. The final chapter of Song of Songs describes love this way:

> For love is as strong as death,
>   passion as fierce as Sheol.
> Its arrows are like arrows of fire,
>   the very flame of the LORD.[3]
> Mighty waters cannot quench love,
>   nor rivers drown it.
> If a man offered all the wealth of his house for love,
>   it would be utterly despised.
>
>   (8:6b–7)

There is something powerful about love that defies rational explanation. When we fall truly, madly, deeply in love, we know with every fiber of our being that no mere biological dissertation on hormones and endorphins and selfish genes will do. There is something supernatural, something spiritual about love that makes the poet's description of it as "the very flame of the LORD" apt. When we fall in love, we know right down to the core of our being that the metaphysical elements that make life worth living—truth and beauty and purpose and meaning—are every bit as real as the physical laws that govern the world. The act of falling in love is a step toward seeking God; pursuing that love through a lifetime of marriage turns that one step into a pathway toward our Creator.

Treasure Sacred Moments

It would take a heart of stone to remain untouched by J. M. Barrie's book and Walt Disney's animated classic *Peter Pan*. The deft appeals to the innocence —complicated innocence, to be sure—of childhood in these works are hard to resist. One of most delightful adaptations of the Peter Pan story is the

Steven Spielberg movie *Hook*, which pits Robin Williams (as Pan) against Dustin Hoffman (as Hook). In this cinematic version of the story, Peter Pan has—ye gods!—grown up. The figure who was once the quintessential mischievous boy has become a neurotic, risk-averse *lawyer*. So thoroughly has Pan (now Peter *Panning*) become an adult that he has forgotten he was ever a boy in Neverland at all. But if Peter had forgotten Neverland, Neverland had not forgotten him. Still bent on revenge over his lost hand, Captain Hook kidnaps his old nemesis' son and daughter, and the man Panning will be forced to rediscover the genius of the boy Pan to rescue them. But even as Panning begins to remember he is Pan, he still remains stubbornly unable to do the one thing that made Peter Pan *Pan*: he cannot fly. Pan's gift of flight was tied to finding his "happy place," and too many years of "adulting" have stolen away any happy place Peter might once have had. It takes a convenient knock on the head for him to finally find that place—truthfully, not a place but a moment—as he remembers the joy that came with the birth of his son.

I leave it to readers to make their own judgments concerning the artistic merits of *Hook* and its predecessors in Disney's movie and Barrie's book. There is something instructive, however, in Spielberg's notion of happy places. It is the rare soul whose life has been so difficult that not even a single moment lifts its head for consideration as a happy place. I know for myself that there are two moments that vie for attention as my happy places. The first has to do with my older son, the second with his younger brother.

Like many couples, I suppose, my wife, Michaela, and I had a plan for the early years of our marriage. We would get married, see the world, live life to the full, and then settle down and have children. We accomplished the first steps of this plan in grand fashion. School took us to New York and Boston, and our love of travel took us several times to Europe and finally to Israel. It was actually on a New Year's Eve at a Bedouin site in the south of Israel that we decided we had accomplished the first stage of our plan. When we returned to the States, we said, it would be time to start a family. But as the months and then years passed by, no children were forthcoming. It didn't help that during the time we were trying so hard to have children, Michaela's sister was having unbridled reproductive success. Seemingly every time her husband looked at her romantically, out popped a child. After years of trying, we had nearly begun to despair that we would ever have children of our own. Words like *adoption* and intimidating acronyms like *IVF* began to pop up in our conversations. And then it happened. A late cycle, a positive test, and at long last, we were expecting.

As it happened, we found out Michaela was pregnant while we were back home in Birmingham for Christmas. Once all the gifts had been distributed, we told my parents we had one "extra" gift for them. We handed each of them a small gift bag in which we had placed an impossibly tiny (and unconscionably expensive) Nike baby shoe. I will never forget the moment when my mom opened the bag. She reached in, took out that little shoe, and held it with a quizzical look. And then it hit her. When she realized what the shoe meant, she literally leapt for joy. No person on earth had prayed harder than my mom for Michaela to conceive, and she wept precious tears of joy at the news. That was indeed a "happy place" moment.

Fast-forward nearly two decades to another such moment. As I finished up my doctoral work and waited (and waited and waited) for an academic position to open up, I served as a Bible teacher at a local Christian high school. I managed to get a university job just before my sons reached high school, so I missed out on the chance to be one of their teachers. I did, however, get invited to return for a chapel service when my younger son was a senior. My son wasn't just any senior, though; he had been voted chaplain for the high school, and that meant he was tapped to introduce me as that day's speaker. No words can suffice to capture the joy of that moment. It was blessing enough just to see my son be the chaplain, but the kindness, honor, and praise he heaped on me as he introduced me—well, no father ever had a prouder moment. I recall saying to him as I walked onto the stage and hugged him, tears streaming down my cheeks, "Dude, you can't do that to me before I have to speak!" But I would take those tears every time for that kind of "happy place" moment. It was a moment I'll never forget it.

In his extraordinary work *The Sabbath*, Abraham Joshua Heschel makes the case that human beings live simultaneously in a realm of time and a realm of space. We are absolute masters of the realm of space. We build and design and perfect *things* with a level of skill that defies the imagination. One need only consider the power and precision of an iPhone to be impressed with humanity's mastery of the realm of space. But our marvelous competence in the realm of space is matched by an equally profound *incompetence* in the realm of time. Time, to us, is ethereal, elusive, and insubstantial. One day seems to drag on forever; another slips past in an instant. And all the while, each *today* slides into the oblivion of *yesterday* with a pace so fearsome that we come to dread the future and even *time* altogether. As Heschel puts it:

> We know what to do with space but do not know what to do about time, except to make it subservient to space. Most of us seem to labor for the sake of things of space. As a result we suffer from a deeply rooted dread of time and stand aghast when compelled to look into its face.[4]

It is our fear of time that pushes us toward a fatal mistake:

> Shrinking, therefore, from facing time, we escape for shelter to things of space. The intentions we are unable to carry out we deposit in space; possessions become the symbols of our repressions, jubilees of frustrations.[5]

When Qoheleth despaired of finding meaning after death, he argued we should embrace the moments of joy God had allotted to us. But there exists a ready counterfeit to moments of joy that often seduces us into its embrace instead. We are sorely tempted to imagine that possessions are our source of happiness, that accumulating things is the same as experiencing moments of joy. But once again, from Heschel: "Things, when magnified, are forgeries of happiness, they are a threat to our very lives; we are more harassed than supported by the Frankensteins of spatial things."[6]

Accumulating possessions is not the same as experiencing moments of joy. Qoheleth tells us he accumulated "things" with an eagerness few could match. Vineyards, gardens, parks, fruit trees, pools, slaves, flocks, herds, silver, gold, musicians, delights of the flesh, concubines—all of these he collected (2:4–8). He boasts, "Whatever my eyes desired I did not refuse them; I did not hold back my heart from any pleasure" (v. 10). But then he reflects:

> Then I considered all the works that my hands had accomplished, and the toil that I had toiled to do so, and behold, it was nothing more than vanity and chasing after the wind. Nothing was gained under the sun.
> (v. 11)

Qoheleth doesn't counsel accumulating wealth as an antidote to the problem of mortality. Wealth may provide a measure of comfort, but it often creates worry and anxiety as well (5:10–16). His guidance is to embrace joyous moments rather than supposedly joyous possessions. Each of the "eat and drink and enjoy what is good" passages mentioned above (cf. 2:24–25; 3:13; 5:18; 8:15) includes a time element alongside it. These are moments to embrace "during the few days of life that God gives a person as their lot" (5:18). Possessions too readily delude us into thinking they are the products of our own effort and ingenuity; *moments* are precious gifts from God. We will find God's presence more readily in joyous moments than in whatever "things" might try to take their place.

Conclusion

In a chapter on joy, one word of caution is in order. Just as possessions are no substitute for moments of joy, neither is decadence. The Teacher both cheers on and cautions at the same time:

> Rejoice, young man, during your youth, and let your heart cheer you in the days when you are young. Follow the paths of your heart and pursue what your eyes see, *but know this as well: all these things God will bring to judgment.*
> (11:9)

In what may well be a postscript to the original work, we find this similar warning in the book's closing lines:

> Fear God and keep his commandments, for this applies to all of humanity. For God will bring every deed into judgment, even every secret thing whether good or bad.
> (12:13b–14)

Excess, whether in the form of greed or of debauchery, is a counterfeit of true joy. It offers a momentary frisson of bliss but robs us in return of genuine, long-lasting joy. If we want to find God's blessing in the gifts he has provided us, we must content ourselves with those things that are actually *his* gifts and not mere substitutes.

Conclusion: Seeking God in Christ

Back to the Beginning

I BEGAN THIS STUDY WITH THOUGHTS about the death of my dear friend Jim Barnette. From that first difficult phone call that warned something was terribly wrong to the devastating announcement of his fatal diagnosis two months later to his death just a few months later still—these were moments in which God seemed not just elusive but absent altogether. The days of Jim's physical suffering were mercifully short, but the rapidity with which he was taken from us was both blessing and curse. We blinked our eyes, and he was gone.

I am sure Jim must have wrestled through his own times of anger and lament over the way his days were suddenly cut short. Somehow, though, he managed to keep encouraging the rest of us, even as he knew he would soon leave us behind. In a letter sharing the news concerning his condition, he wrote:

> While we are heartbroken by this diagnosis, we realize that God is always with us. And because of the death and resurrection of our Lord and Savior, Jesus Christ, we have not been defeated. Actually, just the contrary . . . death has lost the battle. As I always declare on Easter Sunday morning from Brookwood's pulpit, "Tomb's Empty!" and it still is today.

Jim's words were and are a poignant reminder of one last and most important place where we should seek an elusive God: *in his Son*. Jim faced death with the assurance of the resurrection, with confidence in Christ's empty tomb. Even in his last days, Jim urged us to seek God by seeking Christ.

Seeking God Alongside Christ

As we have considered ways to seek our elusive God, we have worked through a number of paths that lie before us and that beckon us to continue our search: Scripture, nature, humanity, worship, silence, doubt, suffering, death, joy. The life and words of Jesus connect with each one of these paths to God.

Scripture

The words of Scripture were never far from the mouth of Jesus. When challenged by various opponents, his ready reply was "Have you not read?"[1] and he directed his hearers to signposts in the Scriptures that would lead them to eternal life and to himself (Matt 19:16–19; Mark 14:49; Luke 24:27, 32, 45; John 5:39). Jesus also recognized the challenges that Scripture poses. In his "You have heard . . . , but I say . . . " sayings in the Sermon on the Mount, he acknowledged that Scripture could be complicated, and he charted a path for working through its tensions. Ultimately, he went through with the cross rather than seeking escape because he knew it was the path that the Scriptures had charted for his life (Matt 26:54–56).

Nature

Jesus regarded the sun that rose on both the evil and the good and the rain that fell on both the just and the unjust as signs of God's goodness (Matt 5:45). He marveled at the beauty of God's creation, evident in something as simple as a lily; he insisted that "not even Solomon in all his glory was clothed like one of these" (Matt 6:28–29). Jesus also acknowledged the brokenness of creation that marred its beauty, and he looked forward to creation's ultimate redemption. As he walked on the waters and calmed the winds and the waves, Jesus laid down markers of hope and promise that he would one day vanquish the hostile waters of Genesis 1 and usher in a new world in which there would be "no more sea" (Rev 21:1).

Humanity

Jesus was a persistent critic of those who refused to devote themselves fully to God. He repeatedly cried out, "You of little faith!" when his hearers remained unwilling to believe. He asked Peter, "Why did you doubt?" when he wavered on the sea, and he chastised his disciples for all manner of shortcomings. And yet, Jesus never lost his love for humanity. He marveled over the faith of those who did believe as often as he criticized those who did not. A centurion concerned about his servant (Matt 8:10; Luke 7:9), friends who brought a paralytic to him (Matt 9:2; Mark 2:5; Luke 5:20), a woman who sought healing just by touching the hem of Jesus' garment (Matt 9:22; Mark 5:34; Luke 8:48), a blind man on the road to Jericho (Matt 9:29; Mark 10:52; Luke 18:42), a Canaanite woman who sought relief for her tormented daughter (Matt 15:28; Mark 7:29), a tearful woman who silently bathed his feet (Luke 7:50)—all of these were commended for their faith rather than rebuked for unbelief. He saw a vision of the kingdom of God in the faces of little children (Matt 19:14; Mark 10:14; Luke 18:16), praised a poor widow who donated her two small copper coins (Mark 12:43-44), and even imagined that a Samaritan could serve as an example for others to follow (Luke 10:25-37). Jesus recognized our frailty, but he still saw us as bearers of the image of God.

Worship

Jesus demonstrated the importance of worship as he continued to follow the rituals that had preserved his people over the centuries. When he visited his hometown of Nazareth, "he went up to the synagogue on the sabbath day *as was his custom*" (Luke 4:16). When he healed a leper, he ordered him to show himself to the priest and offer the gift Moses had commanded (Matt 8:1-4; Mark 1:40-44; Luke 5:12-14). He journeyed to Jerusalem each year at Passover (John 2, 6, 11), worshiped in the temple, and grew angry when God's house was misused (Matt 12:12-13; Mark 11:15-17; Luke 19:45-46; John 2:14-17). Jesus also saw the value of worshiping in community with others. He pressed his followers to love one another just as he had loved them (John 13:34), and he assured them he would be present with them whenever two or three were gathered in his name (Matt 18:20).

Silence

Jesus began his ministry with his own wilderness experience (Matt 4:1-11; Mark 1:12-13; Luke 4:1-13). For forty days, he suffered the privations of the desert, and he suffered these privations alone. Angels eventually came to minister to him but only after his wilderness sojourn had ended. As he endured the powerful temptations of the evil one, he did so by himself, armed only with the words of Scripture. Throughout his ministry, Jesus was inundated by crowds seeking instruction or healing or food, but he never ceased trying to find moments and places of solitude where he could be alone with God (Matt 14:23; Mark 1:35; 6:46; Luke 5:16; 6:12).

Doubt

Jesus experienced doubt as perhaps no other person ever has. At Gethsemane, he expressed full confidence in God's greatness, saying, "Father, for you all things are possible." But his trust in God's goodness was sorely tested as he begged to be released from the cross and was refused (Matt 26:39, 42; Mark 14:36, 39; Luke 22:42–44). He continued to wrestle with God's goodness on the cross as he cried out, "My God, my God, why have you forsaken me?" (Matt 27:46; Mark 15:34). And yet, even in the midst of excruciating doubt, Jesus kept pressing on toward God. Despite his doubts, he never wavered on his journey.

Suffering

What more need be said about the suffering of Jesus given the centrality of the cross in Christian belief and practice? The passion of the Christ—his travail in the garden, his arrest, trials, scourging, mocking, and crucifixion culminating in Easter Sunday—is remembered each year in the most important week in the Christian calendar. One more item might be added though. Jesus suffered not only on the cross and in the events immediately leading up to it; he also suffered simply in his becoming human. Paul tells us that although Christ Jesus existed as God, he set aside his divine prerogatives, humbling himself, and becoming human, all on our behalf (Phil 2:5–8). He suffered the limitations of human existence—hunger and thirst, weakness and fatigue, temptations and trials, wounds and finally death—just as we do. Jesus suffered not just in dying for us but in living for us as well.

Death

Jesus' prayers in the garden stand as witness to the fact that he didn't want to die. He begged the Father to "remove this cup" from him, to excuse him from his impending crucifixion. But in the end, he embraced his death when he saw it was not God's will to spare his life. Alone at Gethsemane, with his disciples asleep some distance away, Jesus could have slipped away quietly, hiked a mile or so over the Mount of Olives, and disappeared into the wilderness never to be seen again. But he didn't. He set his face toward the cross and allowed himself to be arrested, tortured, and killed. Though he cried out in confusion when it seemed God had abandoned him, he also cried out at his death, "Father, into your hands I commit my spirit" (Luke 23:46).

Joy

Jesus saw the hand of God in sun and rain and flowers and children (Matt 5:45; 6:28; 18:3; 19:14; Mark 10:14; Luke 12:27; 18:16). He found joy in being with other people. He called a group of people to himself, poured his life into them, loved them, and ultimately called them "friends" (John 15:13–15). He turned water into wine for a wedding (John 2:1–11), and he ate and drank so often with the lost souls he was trying to reach that his enemies derided him as a glutton and a drunkard (Matt 11:19; Luke 7:34). He looked forward to times of feasting with his disciples (Luke 22:15), and he looked forward with the same sense of anticipation to a time when he would feast with all of his people (Matt 8:11; Luke 13:29).

Jesus pursued and called his followers to pursue all of these varied paths toward God. He showed the way and beckoned us to follow in his footsteps.

Jesus Must Also Be Sought

Throughout this study, we have considered the twin notions of God's deliberate elusiveness and God's earnest desire for humanity to seek after him. Envisioning a time of exile for the nation, Moses warns that God's people will be scattered among the nations and forced to serve other gods. But when they find themselves in exile, he counsels, "If you seek the LORD your God, you will find him, if you pursue him with all your heart and all your soul" (Deut 4:29). Jeremiah voices similar thoughts as he relays the divine message: "If you seek me, you will find me, if you pursue me with all your heart" (29:13). In our own time of spiritual exile, it falls to us as well to seek God even as he remains elusive.

Here, it bears noting that Jesus, too, must be sought, for he also remains elusive. Though Jesus had come to earth as a man and had embraced the weaknesses and limitations allotted to human beings, he still refused to be pinned down, hemmed in, or "domesticated." When Jesus' fellow townspeople in Nazareth grew angry at his sermon and attempted to hurl him off a nearby cliff, he simply passed right through their midst and went on his way (Luke 4:30). When religious authorities tried to arrest him for this word of teaching or that, he remained untouchable "for his hour had not yet come" (John 7:25–30; 8:20; cf. 8:58; 10:31–39). He taught in parables as much to obscure his message from those who were not committed as to enlighten those who were (Matt 13:10–17). In his conversations with individuals, he was often deliberately cryptic. He mystified Nicodemus with talk of being born again (John 3), confused the woman at the well with his reference to living water (John 4), and amazed Pilate with his evasive answers about who he was and what claims he had made (Matt 27:11–14; Mark 15:2–5). Even the incarnation itself is an act of purposeful elusiveness. Though he could have come as a king, a demigod, or simply his true transfigured self, Jesus took on the form of a helpless baby, a growing boy, and a misunderstood man. It was never obvious and undeniable that he was God in human flesh.

At this stage of our study, it should be clear why Jesus revealed himself in such a "present but elusive" manner: As with the Father, so the Son must be sought. Jesus spoke in evasive terms to Nicodemus and the woman at the well *to urge them to take the next step* in pursuit of the one with whom they were speaking. He wanted the Syro-Phoenician woman to pursue not just healing for her daughter but the healer himself (Matt 15:22–28). He wanted the rich young ruler to pursue not just eternal life but himself, the giver of eternal life (Matt 19:21). It wasn't enough to seek the things *around* Jesus—Judas did this; James and John did this as they sought the best seats in the kingdom (Mark 10:37); the multitudes did this as they searched for healing or food. Jesus insisted that we follow *him*. At the risk of losing family and wealth and status and comfort, those who would seek an elusive God must seek *Jesus*.

Hold On in Hope

There are few more moving scenes in Scripture than that of the conversation between Jesus and the so-called thief on the cross (cf. Luke 23:39–43). The men who suffered crucifixion alongside Jesus were actually not thieves but rebels against Rome. Matthew's term for the pair, *lēstai*, has in mind "revolutionaries," precisely the sort of individuals for whom crucifixion was reserved. While one of the two men mocked Jesus and prodded him to save himself if he was actually the Messiah, the other addressed Jesus in a quite different fashion. He appealed to him in the simplest of terms: "Remember me when you come into your kingdom." It is Jesus' response that is so important for us. Nailed to a cross, bearing the wounds of Rome's soldiers on his body, doomed to die, Jesus said, "I tell you truly, today you shall be with me in paradise." In his darkest moment, a moment when he might well have succumbed to his doubts and simply given up, Jesus held on in hope. Despite his circumstances, indeed in defiance of his circumstances, Jesus refused to let go.

I am jealous of those who seem to slip lightly by the sorts of spiritual doubts that stand like Scylla and Charybdis in the course of my own voyage of faith. My heart longs for some explanation for why the world is the way the world is, but I am not convinced there is any such explanation to be had before I shuffle off this mortal coil. I have accepted the fact that it will be a difficult road that leads ultimately to my Creator. And, truthfully, I've made peace with that decision. I have nowhere else to go. With Peter, I can only say, "Lord, to whom *could* we go? You are the one who has the words of eternal life" (John 6:67–68). But at the same time that I admit that a difficult road of seeking lies ahead, I take confidence and inspiration from the courage and example of my friend whose sufferings prompted the writing of this book. In a letter to a friend who mourned the recent loss of her sister, John Muir wrote:

> However clear our faith and hope and love, we must suffer—but with glorious compensation. While death separates, it unites, and the Sense of loneliness grows less and less as we become accustomed to the new light, communing with those who have gone on ahead in spirit, and feeling their influence as if again present in the flesh. Your own experience tells you this, however. The Source of all Good turns even sorrow and seeming separation to our advantage, makes us better, drawing us closer together in love, enlarging, strengthening, brightening our views of the spirit world and our hopes of immortal union. Blessed it is to know and feel, even at this cost, that neither distance nor death can truly separate those who love.[2]

These tender words work to assuage the grief we feel at the loss of someone so dear to us. He added in closing:

> In His strength we must live on, work on, doing the good that comes to heart and hand, looking forward to meeting in that City which the streams of the River of Life make glad.

There is a great deal of comfort in words like these for those who hold on in faith to the belief that our searching will one day be finding when we, at last, are called into God's presence.

To these I would add words of comfort from my friend. Each Sunday, Jim Barnette borrowed these words from his own childhood pastor and offered them as his benediction for the congregation he pastored. They are the words that closed his own final letter to those of us who loved him so much:

> Depart now, In the Fellowship of God the Father,
> And as you Go, Remember:
> By the *Goodness* of God
> You were born into this World;
> By the *Grace* of God
> You have been kept all the day long,
> Even until this hour;
> And by the *Love* of God,
> Fully revealed in the Face of Jesus,
> You have been Redeemed, and
> You are *Being Redeemed*. Amen.[3]

Notes

Introduction

1. John Milton, "On His Blindness," in *The Poetical Works of John Milton* (New York: Frederick A. Stokes & Brother, 1888), 89.

2. Unless otherwise noted, all translations of the Bible are my own. I have taken the liberty of adding italics in various places to emphasize particular elements in the biblical text.

Chapter 1

1. The Deuteronomist, like the Elohist, consistently calls the location of Israel's wilderness encounter with God "Horeb" rather than "Sinai."

2. The Bible preserves more than one set of traditions concerning the nature and function of the tabernacle or tent shrine. The Torah's priestly accounts place the tabernacle at the center of the camp and emphasize its role as a place of sacrifice (cf. Num 1–2). The Elohistic portions of the Torah place the tent on the outskirts of the camp and describe it as a place for oracular utterances rather than sacrifice (cf. Exod 33:7–11).

3. The preparation of the materials for the tabernacle and the manner of its construction are described in elaborate detail in Exod 25–31, 35–40. Further details are found in Lev 1–16 and Num 1–10.

4. The stirring exodus language at the end of Ps 77 appears to serve a similar function (cf. vv. 11–20). The first half of the psalm laments over God's seemingly endless abandonment of the psalmist (cf. vv. 1–10). The psalmist's recollection of the exodus may serve here to press home the point that God certainly could rescue the psalmist—he did so on a grand scale in the past for the psalmist's ancestors—but for some reason, he chooses not to come to the psalmist's aid today.

5. It seems clear that Pss 42–43 were originally one psalm containing three stanzas. Note that Ps 43 is the only psalm in this section that lacks a superscription and that it shares the same refrain (v. 5) as that found in Ps 42 (vv. 5, 11).

6. The Hebrew is uncertain here. The phrase may mean "set counsel in my soul," perhaps as a colloquial expression for experiencing feelings of anxiety. In light of the parallel phrase "pain in my heart" in the following line, the translation here follows the emendation of the Masoretic Text's *'ēṣôṯ* ("counsel") to *'aṣṣāḇôṯ* ("wounds")—a change of only one letter in the consonantal text.

Chapter 2

1. The name "Areopagus" is Greek for "hill of Ares." Those familiar with the King James Version will recall the translation of the same place as "Mars Hill," a rendering that reflects the fact that Mars was the Roman equivalent of the Greek deity Ares. Metonymically, the Areopagus could also refer to the Athenian tribunal, the Council of the Areopagus. Luke's description of the scene in vv. 22a and 33 suggests he has in mind the tribunal rather than the hill.

2. In an earlier era, the Deuteronomist suggested that God divided humanity into nations, assigning the nations to the various gods but keeping Israel for himself. Thus, the so-called Song of Moses declares, "When the Most High apportioned the nations, when he divided the sons of men, he fixed the borders of the peoples according to the numbers of the gods. But YHWH's portion was his people; Jacob was his allotted inheritance" (Deut 32:8–9; cf. 4:19). Passages like Ps 82:6–7—"I said you were gods . . . but you shall die like mortals"—mark the theological transition that ultimately finds expression in Paul's language in Acts 17.

3. Careful readers of Ezekiel's vision will note the heavy emphasis these visions place on mobility. In his vision in ch. 1, for example, the prophet repeatedly mentions the wings of his visionary creatures, their rapid, lightning-like movements, and even the wheels upon which they were set (cf. vv. 5–21). These cherubim and the wheels they ride are depicted as carrying the divine presence; when it proves necessary, they will carry it away from Zion (cf. Ezek 10).

4. Note that a marked ambivalence concerning the temple remains even in the New Testament. Jesus, of course, famously cleanses the temple with whip in hand (Matt 21:12–13; Mark 11:15–17; Luke 19:45–46; John 2:13–22) and announces that the temple itself will soon be destroyed (Matt 24:2; Mark 13:2; Luke 21:6). Later, Stephen's sermon in Acts 7 reaches its crescendo when he appears to criticize Solomon's temple essentially as an idol (cf. vv. 46–50).

5. Gilgamesh, Tablet XI.161–63. Tablet XI of the Gilgamesh Epic draws the story of the Flood from the Akkadian myth called "Atrahasis." Both texts preserve this description of the gods' swarming like flies around the sacrifices of the "Babylonian Noah," known as Atrahasis or Ut-Napishtim.

6. Similar sentiments are expressed in Jer 6:20; Mic 6:6–8; Ps 40:6; and in various other passages.

Chapter 3

1. Lexicographers are largely in agreement that the noun *tôrā(h)* derives from a verbal root **yrh* (originally **wrh*). Unfortunately, more than one such verbal root is preserved in Hebrew. One root, **yrh* I, has the meaning "to throw, cast"; another, **yrh* III, means "to teach, instruct." The editors of HALOT (*Hebrew and Aramaic Lexicon of the Old Testament*) suggest the directional and instructional aspects of these two roots are connected in the notion of pointing out the right route. Others have suggested a connection with the Akkadian word *têrtu*, relating to a divine oracle.

2. J. R. R. Tolkien, *The Fellowship of the Ring: Being the first part of the Lord of the Rings* (Boston: Houghton Mifflin, 2002), 72.

3. I follow Steinbeck's rendering of the term here, though the Hebrew term in Gen 4:7 is actually *timshol*.

4. John Steinbeck, *East of Eden* (New York: Penguin, 2002), 302.

5. Jacob Milgrom, *Leviticus*, 3 vols. (New York: Doubleday, 1991–2001).

6. The expression "in the hearing" is, in Hebrew, literally "in the ears" of the people.

7. It seems likely that, in its original context, the septennial reading of "this Torah" envisioned by Deut 31:10–11 would have referred only to the book of Deuteronomy or a portion of it.

Chapter 4

1. The Hebrew word *qawwām* found in the Masoretic Text is quite difficult. With the editors of *HALOT* and the translators of the NRSVue, I find it likely that the text should be emended to *qôlām*. The MT form may be simply a copyist's error, though it is also possible that a scribe changed the form deliberately to avoid a contradiction between v. 3 (Heb 4), "Their voice is not heard," and v. 4 (Heb 5), "Their voice goes out to all the earth." It is not necessary, however, to regard vv. 3 and 4 as contradictory. The psalmist's assertion is that, though the heavens do not speak with words, their voice does in fact go out to all the world.

2. Of particular interest in Ps 19 is the fact that in the second half of the psalm, the psalmist turns from the grandeur of God's creation to the grandeur of God's law. It is the juxtaposition of these two that underscores the fact that both Scripture and creation are means of God's self-revelation.

3. As delightful a language as English is, it is far too wordy to capture the terse turns of phrase found in Hebrew poetry. Proverbs expresses the notion above in only four words: *niḇhār šēm mēʿōšer rāḇ*, "to-be-chosen a-name than-wealth great." The Preacher in Qoheleth is similarly brief: *ṭôḇ šēm miššemen ṭôḇ*, "good a-name than-oil good."

4. See, for example, 2 Sam 12:15, Sir 1:12. Note the Akkadian cognate *enēšu*, "to be weak, dilapidated."

5. Interestingly, v. 11 is written in Aramaic, a language related to Hebrew much as Portuguese is to Spanish. Of the 929 chapters of the Old Testament, 920 are written in Hebrew; only nine chapters and a few scattered verses like the one here are written in Aramaic.

6. Tolkien, *The Return of the King: Being the third part of The Lord of the Rings* (Boston: Houghton Mifflin, 2002), 1028–29.

7. William Frederic Badè, *The Life and Letters of John Muir* (Boston: Houghton Mifflin, 1924), 241.

8. John Muir, *My First Summer in the Sierra* (Boston: Houghton Mifflin, 1911), 49.

9. John Muir, interview by French Strother in "Three Days with John Muir," *World's Work* 17 (1909): 11355–58.

10. Muir, *First Summer*, 60.

11. Shavuot is, perhaps, more commonly known to Christians as Pentecost. A numerical element is present in both the Hebrew and the Greek names for the festival. Shavuot means literally "weeks" and derives its name from the seven weeks of the barley harvest that begin with the feast of Unleavened Bread and end at Shavuot. The Greek name "Pentecost" is, literally, "fifty," again denoting the day after the seven weeks of seven days are complete.

Chapter 5

1. The passages listed in this section all make use of either the nominal or verbal forms of the Hebrew root *'zr*.

2. The Greek translation of the Hebrew Bible known as the Septuagint (abbreviated as LXX, reflecting the fact that the Latin "septuaginta" means "seventy") contains what scholars describe as a "pious correction" to indicate that humans are created a little lower than *angels* (cf. Heb 2:7–9).

3. The Hebrew phrase *nôrā'ōṯ niplêṯî* is somewhat difficult. *nôrā'ōṯ* is a *niphal* participle from the verb **yr'*, meaning "to be feared, dreaded, or awesome." Here, it acts as an adverb modifying the verb *niplêṯî*, which, despite the loss of a quiescent aleph, appears to derive from **pl'*. As another *niphal* form, *niplêṯî* apparently means "to be wonderful."

4. Charles Dickens, *A Tale of Two Cities* (1859; Toronto: Bantam Books, 1985), 366–68.

5. There are also echoes of Sydney Carton in J. K. Rowling's portrayal of Severus Snape. Like Carton, the facade of Snape's personality is unsavory, but a much better person lies beneath the surface. Snape is a rival with James Potter for the affections of Lily, the woman who would become James' wife. Though Snape is unable to save his direct rival, James, he does give his life to save James' son, Harry. And in the years after this sacrifice, Harry preserves Snape's memory by naming his son Albus (after Dumbledore) Severus (after Snape) Potter.

6. J. R. R. Tolkien, *The Two Towers: Being the second part of The Lord of the Rings* (Boston: Houghton Mifflin Company, 2002), 416.

7. In what seems a far different era culturally, a movie like Disney's 1967 film *The Jungle Book* could even quote John 15:13 as Bagheera spoke in honor of Balloo's (seeming!) sacrifice of his life to save Mowgli from Shere Khan.

8. Richard Selzer, *Mortal Lessons: Notes on the Art of Surgery* (New York: Simon & Schuster, 1976), 46.

Chapter 6

1. Concerning Shiloh, see Josh 18, 1 Sam 1, Jer 7, and Ps 78:60.

2. When Jeroboam sets up his golden calves in Dan and Bethel, he declares, "Behold your gods, O Israel, who brought you up from the land of Egypt" (1 Kgs 12:28). Jeroboam's reference to the exodus highlights the fact that he wasn't actually calling the Israelites to worship foreign gods; he was encouraging them to worship the right God (YHWH) but in the wrong way (in the form of the calves). In Exod 32, despite the fact that Aaron makes only one golden calf, he utters the same words—identical save for the use of "these" instead of "behold"—as Jeroboam: "These are your gods, O Israel, who brought you up from the land of Egypt" (v. 4). The incongruous use of the plural in Aaron's case suggests that the golden calf account intends to strike at more than one target. Aaron's calf is condemned, to be sure, but the author also has his sights trained on Jeroboam's calves. Note that inappropriate worship rather than the worship of foreign gods is also the issue at Sinai, as Aaron couples veneration of the calf with the words, "Tomorrow shall be a festival to YHWH."

3. The Hebrew phrase *bassāḵ 'eddaddēm*, rendered here as "with the throng" and "walk in procession," is quite difficult. For a discussion of the passage see Peter C. Craigie, *Psalms 1–50*, WBC 19 (Waco: Word, 1983), 324.

4. See, for example, Gerhard von Rad, *The Problem of the Hexateuch and Other Essays*, trans. E.W. Trueman Dicken (New York: McGraw Hill, 1966), 3, 56.

5. See especially Isa 53.

6. *Fauda*, season 1, episode 12, directed by Assaf Bernstein, written by Lior Raz, Avi Issacharoff, and Moshe Zonder, aired May 3, 2015.

Chapter 7

1. London receives, on average, 23 inches of rain per year, and Seattle 39 inches; the Upper Galilee receives an average of 44 inches per year.

2. The account of Moses' early life is found in Exod 2–4.

Chapter 8

1. This is not an unreasonable question, given the fact that the Israelites in Exod 1–2 descend into bitter slavery and genocide with very little intervention on God's part.

2. The Hebrew of the first colon is somewhat ambiguous. One could understand the phrase *bal yidrōš* to refer to the wicked, meaning "the wicked do not seek." What the wicked fail to seek, however, is left unspecified in the text. Alternatively, the phrase could refer to God, suggesting the wicked believe "God will not seek," that is, God will not seek out their evil behavior. Against this reading is the fact that the text doesn't specify this as either the thought or the speech of the wicked. It is noteworthy, however, that the similar expression, *lō' tidrōš*, in v. 13 does refer specifically to God and the fact that the wicked believe God won't seek out their crimes.

3. Concerning the verb "seduce," see Exod 22:5. For "overpower," see Deut 22:25.

4. Mother Teresa, *Come Be My Light: The Private Writings of the "Saint of Calcutta,"* edited with commentary by Brian Kolodiejchuk, M.C. (New York: Doubleday, 2007).

5. These sentiments were expressed in a letter to the Rev. Michael van der Peet dated September 22, 1979, in *Come Be My Light*, 288.

6. *Come Be My Light*, 186. This is only a brief selection of a paper Teresa included in a July 3, 1959, letter to Father Lawrence Trevor Picachy, who was then serving as rector of St. Xavier's Calcutta and would later rise to the rank of archbishop and then cardinal.

Chapter 9

1. Note that it is always *the* Satan in the book, indicating perhaps a name or a title meaning "the Adversary."

2. The reference to Satan in 1 Chr 21:1 stands out from the appearances in Zechariah and Job, not only because it lacks the definite article—it is just "Satan," not "the Satan"—but also because of the action attributed to Satan. In 2 Sam 24:1, we are told that God's anger was kindled against Israel, "and he incited David against them, saying, 'Go and number Israel and Judah.'" The text is particularly odd as this divinely prompted census is followed by repentance on David's part and punishment on God's part. In 1 Chr 21:1, we find a parallel to the text in 2 Sam 24. In 1 Chr 21:1, we find a parallel to the text in 2 Sam 24; in the Chronicler's version, however, it is Satan—not God—who incites David to take the census. This sort of attribution of a theologically problematic action on God's part to Satan becomes much more pronounced in the Second Temple period. See, for example, the actions of "Mastema," a figure who appears to be equivalent to Satan in Second Temple Jewish books like Jubilees.

3. Job is mentioned as a character of exceptional righteousness in Ezek 14:14, 20. While this reference suggests that the story of righteous Job was well known, it doesn't tell us much about the historicity of Job. This is true, in part, because Job is mentioned alongside Noah and another character listed by Ezekiel as *"Dan'el."* While we might be tempted to connect *Dan'el* with the well-known figure of Daniel,

the two names are not spelled the same way in Hebrew. It seems more likely that Ezekiel's reference is to the well-known figure *Dan'el* from Israel's Canaanite (specifically Ugaritic) neighbors. There is little to suggest *Dan'el* was an actual figure from history, so his mention doesn't advance our understanding of Job's own historicity.

4. A careful reader will note the connection Job makes between his mother's "belly" and the grave. It is not as if Job expects to return to the womb that gave birth to him; he knows he will return instead to the womb-shaped and womb-reminiscent grave.

5. In the Hebrew text of Job, the offensive expression "curse God" is replaced by the pious euphemism "bless God" (cf. 1:5, 11; 2:5, 9).

6. Athalya Brenner, "Job the Pious? The Characterization of Job in the Narrative Framework of the Book," *JSOT* 43 (1989): 44.

7. The description of the Leviathan occupies 40:25–41:26 in the Hebrew text but 41:1–34 in English (Christian) translations. The difference is only one of versification, not content.

8. Similar images are found in passages that don't mention the Leviathan specifically by name (Job 7:12; Ps 148:7) or that refer to a dragon-like creature named "Rahab" (Job 9:13; 26:12; Ps 89:10; Isa 51:9).

9. This is the translation in the NRSVue, ESV, and NIV, for example.

10. Note that the KJV, ERSV, and RSV all have "myself" in italics in recognition of the fact that this word is absent from the underlying Hebrew.

11. There is the interesting possibility that a double entendre is intended in v. 6 as *niḥamtî 'al* can also mean "I am comforted upon." The ambiguous repent/comfort meaning could be a reflection of both the prose prologue ("I am comforted—I know you're there and that your ways are higher than mine.") and the poetic dialogues ("I reject my silence and will lament."). On the expression *nḥm* as "repent concerning," see, for example, Exod 32:12, 14; 1 Chr 21:15; Ps 90:13. For the same expression as "comfort concerning," see 2 Sam 13:39; 1 Chr 19:2; Job 42:11.

12. Samuel E. Balentine, "'My Servant Job Will Pray for You,'" *Theology Today* 4 (2002): 502–18.

13. John Thavis, "Pope Addresses Suffering in Historic Television Appearance," April 22, 2011, https://catholicherald.co.uk/pope-addresses-suffering-in-historic-television-appearance/.

Chapter 10

1. Tolkien, *The Fellowship of the Ring*, 278.

2. The syntax of this verse is quite difficult, especially as it concerns the Hebrew phrase *'ak heḇel yehĕmāyûn*. The translation here follows the verbal form in the Masoretic Text. Others suggest an emendation to the noun *hāmôn*, "turmoil," but this does little to improve the sense of the line.

3. Roy Batty was the replicant played so brilliantly by Rutger Hauer in the 1982 Ridley Scott film. Like the other replicants in *Blade Runner*, Batty was programmed to live only a short while, and the predetermined moment of his death was nearly upon him.

4. One version of the LXX, known as Symmachus, contains a reference to "gods" in v. 9 as well. This witness is followed by the NRSVue, which translates the verse, "Any hope of capturing it will be disappointed; were not even the gods overwhelmed at the sight of it?"

5. See Emanuel Tov, *Textual Criticism of the Hebrew Bible* (Minneapolis: Fortress, 1992), 269.

6. A similar sort of "demotion" of what were formerly thought to be gods can be seen in Psalm 82.

7. Here, Job refers to his mother's womb as "my womb."

8. Although some translations suggest Job's reference is to "*re*building ruins," it seems more likely that the buildings the kings and counselors once built are *now* ruins. Like Shelley's Ozymandias, they thought to build structures that would endure forever, but now they, like their handiwork, are only a memory:

> Nothing beside remains. Round the decay
> Of that colossal Wreck, boundless and bare
> The lone and level sands stretch far away.

9. The name "Abaddon" is derived from a verbal root meaning "to destroy." Its role as a term referring to the underworld is clear from its use in parallel with "Sheol" (Prov 15:11; 27:20; Job 26:6) and "death" (Job 28:22).

10. See, for example, the fourfold repetition of the phrase in Isa 27:1, 2, 12, 13.

11. The Hebrew text in this line is exceedingly difficult and may be corrupt.

12. Robert Herrick, "To the Virgins, to make much of Time," in *The Poetical Works of Robert Herrick*, ed. L. C. Martin (Oxford: Clarendon Press, 1956, 1968), 84.

13. A. E. Housman, "Loveliest of Trees," in *A Shropshire Lad* (New York: John Lane Company, 1896, 1917), 3.

14. Dickens, *A Tale of Two Cities*, 368.

Chapter 11

1. This sort of rewriting of Shakespeare is often incorrectly described as bowdlerization. Thomas Bowdler cut elements from Shakespeare that he deemed bawdy or profane and unsuitable for children; he did not, however, add elements to Shakespeare's works or alter their plots.

2. Tolkien, *The Two Towers*, 720.

3. With many interpreters, I take the concluding *yāh* in the Hebrew *šalhebetyāh* to be a theophoric ending referring to YHWH.

4. Abraham Joshua Heschel, *The Sabbath: Its Meaning for Modern Man* (1951; New York: Farrar, Straus and Giroux, 1984), 5.

5. Heschel, *The Sabbath*, 5.
6. Heschel, *The Sabbath*, 6.

Conclusion

1. Cf. Matt 12:3, 5; 19:4; 21:16; 22:31; Mark 2:25; 12:10, 26; Luke 6:3; 10:26
2. John Muir, letter to Julia Merrill Moores on the death of her sister Kate, July 25, 1900, https://scholarlycommons.pacific.edu/jmcl/14825/.
3. Jim attributed these words to the Rev. Dr. John Claypool of Crescent Hill Baptist Church.

Scripture Index

GENESIS
1   57, 58, 75, 164
1–11   88
1:2   113
1:10–15   55, 56
1:26–28   58
1:27   59
1:27–28   56
2   58, 59
2–3   113
2:7   58
2:8   50
2:9   88
2:15   50, 58
2:18   58
2:19   58
2:19–20   59
2:23   155
2:23–25   59
2:29   59
3:12   61
3:23–24   50
4   133
4:5   38
4:7   34, 173n17
4:13   38
4:17   50, 88
11   50
11:4   50, 88
11:5   50
11:8   50
12:1   89
12:7   133
13:4   133
13:12   50
16   100
16:2   155
17   100
18   25, 100
18:22–33   126
18:25   38
19:16   50
19:20   50
21   86
21:15   86
21:19   86
22:2   38
26:25   133
28:11–22   91
29:20–21   155
29:23   155
29:30   155
30:3   155
30:4   155
30:16   155
31:19–35   47
32   17, 18, 25
32:24   17
32:24–32   91
32:25   18
32:26   18
32:28   18
32:30   18
33:20   133
38:8   155
49:25   58

EXODUS
1–2   175n49
1:13–14   87
2   89
2–4   175n48
2:23   87
3   89, 90
3–4   25, 100
3:7   87
14   76
15   76
15:11   134
15:17   145
16:3   87
16:4   32
17:3   88
18:20   32
19–24   25
22:4   121
22:5   176n51
22:7   121
22:9   121
24   6, 7
24:3   6
24:6–8   6
24:7   35
24:9–11   6
25–31   171n5
32   70
32:4   175n42
32:12   177n65
32:14   177n65
33:3   8
33:7–11   171n4
33:11   8
33:12   89
33:15   8
33:17   8
33:18   8
33:19–23   8
33:23   91
35–40   171n5

LEVITICUS
1–16   133, 171n5
1–27   35
7   151
12:7   156
16   9
20:18   156

Numbers

1–2   171n4
1–10   171n5
11:5   87
12:8   7
20:5   87
20:11 38
21:5   87

Deuteronomy

3:24–25   38
4:11–12   7
4:19   172n10
4:29   167, 168
5:12–15   79
5:23–28   7
5:25–26   7
6:4–5   78
6:6–8   79
6:20–25   74
10:17   134
12:2–3   79
14:3–21   79
14:22–29 79
14:26   152
16:16–17 79
22:13   155
22:25   176n51
25:6   152
26   54, 73, 74
26:1–10   79
26:5   54
26:5–10   73, 152
26:9–10   54
26:11   152
26:21   74
29:13   168
31:9–13   75
31:10–11 35, 173n21
31:30   35
32:8   134
32:8–9   172n10
32:43   134
32:44   35
33:7   58
33:26   58
34   75
34:10   89

Joshua

1:7   32
8:34–35   35
18   175n41

22:5 32
23:6 32

Judges

4   77
5   76

1 Samuel

1   175n41
5   47
15:22a 24

2 Samuel

7:2   20
7:5   20
7:6–7   20
7:11–12   20
7:13   145
12:15   173n25
13:39   177n65
16:21   155
22:7   91, 92
22:17–18 92
24   176n56

1 Kings

2:3   32
2:10   134
3:3   69
4:7   70
4:22–23   70
5:13–14   70
8:27   20, 43
9:11   70
9:15–19   70
11:1–8   69
11:43   134
12:27   70
12:28   175n42
14:20   134
14:31   134
18:21   134
18:35   138
19:2   90
19:4   90
19:11a   91
19:11b–12 91
22:19   6

2 Kings

9:30   147
10:31 32
23:2   36

1 Chronicles

19:2   177n65
21:1   114, 176n56
21:15   177n65

2 Chronicles

6:16   32
18:18   6
34:30   36

Nehemiah

8:5–8   36
8:8   38
10:30   32

Job

1   113
1–2   114, 126
1:1   113, 115, 117
1:3   117
1:5   177n59
1:6–7   116
1:6–12   38
1:8   113, 114, 116, 117
1:9–11   116
1:11   177n59
1:12   116
1:21   122
1:22   122
2:1–2   116
2:1–7   38
2:3   113, 114, 116, 117
2:4–5   116
2:5   177n59
2:6   116
2:8   117
2:8–13   126
2:9   177n59
2:10   122
3   134
3–29   119
3–42   126
3:1–10   123
3:1–42:6 116
3:10   135
3:11–12   135
3:11–26   123
3:13   135
3:13b–19 135
4:7–8   119
7:12   177n62
7:16   131

7:16–19 111	13:1–2 14	74:1–12 112
7:8–10 136	13:3 134	74:12–17 111
8:3–4 119	19 173n23	74:13–14a 111, 112
9:13 177n62	19:1–4a 43	74:13–14 125
9:16–20 124	19:3 173n22	77:1–10 171n6
9:29 132	19:4 173n22	77:11–20 171n6
10:20–22 136	20:2 59	89:6–12 111
11:6 119	22 10	78 77
21:34 132	22:1 10, 118	78:10 32
26:6 178n76	22:2 10	78:60 175n41
26:12 177n62	22:3 10	79:9 59
28:22 178n76	22:4–5 11	82 178n73
35:16 132	22:14–15 11	82:6–7 172n10
37:2 37	22:19 10	84:10 69
38–39 124	28:7 59	86:17 59
38:1–39:30 124	30:10 59	88 118
38:3 126	33:3 78	88:10–12 136
40:4–5 124, 126	33:20 59	88:14 3
40:6–41:34 124	34:11 32	89 112
40:7 126	37:31 37	89:9–10 112
40:10–13 125	37:40 59	89:10 177n62
40:14 125	39:5 131	89:40–53 112
40:15–24 125	39:6 132	89:48 129
41:1–34 125, 177n61	40:6 172n14	90:1 142
41:9 177n71	42 12, 14, 71, 95	90:2 142
41:25 134	42–43 171n7	90:3 142
42:1–6 125	42:1 12, 13, 72, 95	90:4 142
42:4 126	42:3 14, 95	90:4 143
42:6 125, 177n65	42:4 13	90:5–6 143
42:7 119, 120, 126	42:5 72, 95, 171n7	90:9 37, 143
42:7–17 119	42:6 13	90:10 143
42:8 120	42:9 14, 95	90:12 144
42:10 120, 121	42:9–10 13	90:13 177n65
42:11 121, 177n65	42:11 95, 171n7	90:17 145
	43:1–2 13	95:3 134
Psalms	43:3–4 13	96:1 78
1 37	43:5 95, 171n7	98:1 78
1:1 141	44:22–24 118	104 55
1:2 37, 73	44:23–24 3	104:10–11 153
2:4–6 21	46:6 59	104:13 153
8 44, 105	48:8 145	104:14–15 153
8:1 43, 60	50 22	104:24 41
8:3 145	50:8–13 22, 74	104:26 125
8:3–4 44	51:16–17 23	105 77
8:5–6 60	54:4 59	106 77
8:9 43	63:1 17	109:26 59
9:7 145	65:8 55	115:4–7 46
10:1 3, 10, 100, 118	65:9–13 54, 55	115:7 37
10:4 101	66:5 32	115:9–11 59
10:11 10, 101	66:16 32	115:15 47
10:12–13 101	68:9–10 54	118:7 59
10:13 176n50	70:5 59	118:13 59
10:14 10, 59	73:13–14 97	119 32
13:1 118	74 112	119:1 32

119:11 37, 51, 73	2:16 133	41:10 138
119:25 29	2:18–19 133, 149	42:24 32
119:28 29	2:24 155	44 139
119:30 32	2:24–25 150, 160	44:14b–17 45
119:32 32	3:1–8 150	44:24 46
119:86 59	3:11 137, 150	45 138
119:105 32	3:13 150, 155, 160	45:5 134
119:128 33	3:16 150	45:6 134
119:133 33	3:18–21 137	45:18 134
119:173 59	3:19–21 149	45:21 134, 138
121:1–2 59	4:9–12 156	45:22 134
122:1 69	5:10–16 160	47 139
124:8 59	5:17 155	51:11 147
135 77	5:18 151, 160, 161	51:3a 50, 51
136 77	6:1–2 133, 149	51:9 177n62
136:2 134	6:6 155	51:9–10 112
137:1–4 72	7:1 44	52 139
139:7–10 15	7:15 151	53 175n45
139:13–14 60	8:15 151, 160	53:11 138
139:14–16 57	8:16–17 150	55:8–9 5
144:9 78	9:7–9a 155	55:9 37
146:5 59	9:9 140	55:10–11 36
148:7 177n62	11:5 150	59:11 37
149:1 78	11:9 161	62:7 145
	12:1 140, 141	66 139
Proverbs	12:2 141	66:1 43
1:4 25	12:3 141	
3:1–2 25	12:4 141	**Jeremiah**
3:19 145	12:5 141	4:10 101
4:10 25	12:6–7 141	6:20 172n14
5:15 155	12:13b–14 161	7 21, 175n41
5:18–19 156		7:4 21
10:7 145	**Sirach**	7:5–11 21
13:1 25	1:12 173n25	7:12–14 21
15:11 178n76		9:12 32
15:8 23	**Song of Songs**	10:3–5 45, 46
22:1 44	8:6b–7 157	10:11 173n26
27:20 178n76		10:11–12 46
		12:1 101
Qoheleth	**Isaiah**	15:18 102
1:1 131	1:11 23, 74	20:7 102
1:2 131	1:13b 23	20:9 102
1:3 132	2:3 32	20:14–18 102
1:4–7 132	6:1 6, 25	23:24 15
1:9 132	10 139	25:12 139
1:11 133, 149	27:1 112, 125, 178n77	26:14 32
1:13 150	27:2 178n77	30–31 139
1:17–18 133	27:12 178n77	31:12–14 152, 153
2:1 155	27:13 178n77	32:23 32
2:1–11 133	29:13 80	44:10 32
2:4–8 160	31:4 37	44:23 32
2:10 160	38:14 37	51:39 134
2:11 160	40 138	51:57 134

Ezekiel
1:1 6
1:5–21 172n11
8 21
9:3 21
10 172n11
10:19 21
11:23–25 21
14:14 176n57
14:20 176n57
36:33–35 51

Daniel
9:10 32
9:11 32
12:2 134

Hosea
1:9 85
2:5 84
2:8 84
2:11–13 84, 85
2:14–15 85
12:4–6 18

Amos
2:6–8 84
4:1–2 99
5:10–12 84
5:21 99
5:21–24 84
5:22–24 23
8:2 99
9:1 6
9:1–4 99

Micah
4:2 32
6:6–8 172n14

Habakkuk
2:20 83

Zechariah
2:13 83
3:1–2 114

Matthew
1–2 25
4:1–11 166
4:11 93
5:8 7
5:10–12a 122
5:21–26 81
5:27–30 81
5:44–45 55
5:45 62, 154, 164, 167
6:7 76
6:9–13 76
6:28 167
6:28–29 164
8:1–4 165
8:10 165
8:10–11 153
8:11 167
9:2 165
9:22 165
9:29 165
11:19 153, 167
12:3 178n88
12:5 178n88
12:12–13 165
13:3–9 116
13:10–17 168
13:22 53
14 100, 153
14:13 94
14:14 94
14:22–25 94
14:23 94, 166
14:25–33 81
14:31 99
15 153
15:7–9 80
15:22–28 168
15:28 62, 165
17 25
18:1–6 106
18:3 167
18:4 106
18:6 106
18:20 165
19:4 178n88
19:14 62, 165, 167
19:16–19 164
19:16–21 26
19:16–22 81
19:21 168
20:22 103
21:12–13 172n12
21:16 178n88
22:31 178n88
24:2 172n12
26:39 166
26:42 166
26:54–56 164
27:11–14 168
27:46 166
27:48–50 103
28:19 80

Mark
1:12 93
1:12–13 166
1:13 93
1:35 95, 166
1:40 64
1:40–44 165
1:41 64
2:5 165
2:16 153
2:25 178n88
3:9 94
4:3–9 116
5:34 165
6 153
6:46 166
7:29 165
8 153
9 25
9:42 106
10:14 62, 165, 167
10:37 168
10:38 103
10:52 165
11:15–17 165, 172n12
12:10 178n88
12:26 178n88
12:29 78
12:43–44 165
13:2 172n12
14:32b–36 102, 103
14:36 104, 166
14:39 166
14:49 164
15:2–5 168
15:34 166
15:36–37 103
15:37 104

Luke
1–2 25
2:29 137
4:1–13 166
4:16 165
4:29–30 5
4:30 168

5:12–14 165	6 27, 39, 165	17:29 19
5:15–16 95	6:26 39	17:31 47
5:16 166	6:46 7	17:33 172n9
5:20 165	6:48–58 39	18:25 32
5:30 153	6:60 39	18:26 32
6:3 178n88	6:65 39	19:9 32
6:12 166	6:67–68 27, 169	19:23 32
7:9 165	6:68 39	22:15 47
7:34 153, 167	7:25–30 168	22:16 80
7:36–50 62	8:20 168	22:20 47
7:50 165	8:58 168	23:11 47
8:5–8 116	10 153	24:14 32
8:48 165	10:11 106	24:22 32
9 25, 153	10:14–15 106	
10 62	10:31–39 168	**Romans**
10:25–37 165	11 165	1:19–20 44, 105
10:26 178n88	13:1 106	2:6–7 62
10:30 115	13:34 165	6:3–4 80
10:31–33 116	14:9 61	8:19–23 113
12:18 53	15:13 64, 106, 174n39	14:13 106
12:27 167	15:13–15 167	16:16 80
13:29 153, 167	17:18 62	
15 116	17:21 62	**1 Corinthians**
15:11 115	17:23 62	8:9–11 107
17:2 106	19:28–30 103	10:21 80
18:16 62, 165, 167	20:25 109	11:1–16 80
18:42 165	20:27 109	11:20–34 80
19:8–9 62	20:29 26, 109	12:13 80
19:45–46 165, 172n12		13:7 67
20:9 115	**Acts**	13:12 117
21:1–4 62	1:8 47	14:26 80
21:6 172n12	2:32 47	16:20 80
22:15 153, 167	2:42 80	
22:42–44 166	3:15 47	**2 Corinthians**
23:34 62	5:32 47	3:14 36
23:39–43 169	7:46–50 172n12	4:6 62
23:46 123, 167	7:48 42	13:12 80
24 29, 30	9 25	
24:25–27 30	10:2 62	**Galatians**
24:27 38, 164	10:39–41 47	1:17 92
24:30–31 30	13:15 36	3:27 80
24:32 30, 164	13:31 47	
24:38 99	14:8–18 44, 45	**Ephesians**
24:45 164	14:15a 45	4:5 80
	14:15b–17 45	5:14 77
John	14:17 55	5:19 80
1:18 6, 7	17 18, 172n10	6:18 80
2 165	17:11 31	
2:1–11 153	17:16 47	**Philippians**
2:13–22 172n12	17:22–23 18, 19	2:5–7 65
2:14–17 165	17:22a 172n9	2:5–8 166
3 168	17:24–25 19, 21, 22, 74	
4 168	17:26 19	
5:39 164	17:27–28 19	

2:6–8   77
4:6   80
4:8   62

Colossians
2:12   80
3:16   80
4:2   80

1 Thessalonians
5:26   80

1 Timothy
2:1–8   80
3:16   75
4:13   36, 80
6:16   7

2 Timothy
2:11–13   74
4:2   80

Titus
2:15   80
3:4–8a   74

Hebrews
2:7–9   174n34
4:15   104
10:25   80
11   99
12:1a–2   123

James
1:2–3   122
1:5–8   99
2:19   31
3:7–8   99
4:4   99
4:9   99
5:1   99
5:5   99
5:13   80
5:13–18   80
5:14   80

1 Peter
1:6–7   122
1:8–9   109, 139
2:22–25   77
5:14   80

2 Peter
3:15–16   38

1 John
4:12   7

3 John
11   7

Revelation
19:7–9   153
21:1   164
21:4   123
22:1–2   51